Dharma path

The Secret way to manifestation

Lalit Kumar Numberdar

AF517543

BlueRose ONE.com
Stories Matter
New Delhi • London

BLUEROSE PUBLISHERS
India | U.K.

Copyright © Lalit Kumar Numberdar 2025

All rights reserved by author. No part of this publication may be reproduced, stored in a retrieval system or transmitted in any form or by any means, electronic, mechanical, photocopying, recording or otherwise, without the prior permission of the author. Although every precaution has been taken to verify the accuracy of the information contained herein, the publisher assumes no responsibility for any errors or omissions. No liability is assumed for damages that may result from the use of information contained within.

BlueRose Publishers takes no responsibility for any damages, losses, or liabilities that may arise from the use or misuse of the information, products, or services provided in this publication.

For permissions requests or inquiries regarding this publication, please contact:

BLUEROSE PUBLISHERS
www.BlueRoseONE.com
info@bluerosepublishers.com
+91 8882 898 898
+4407342408967

ISBN: 978-93-7310-327-3

Cover Design: Aman Sharma
Typesetting: Manisha Rawat

First Edition: November 2025

Introduction

In The first part of book "Dharma Path: The Journey of Success," we explored the ten characteristics of Dharma—Dhriti, Kshama, Daman, Asteya, Shaucha, Indriyanigraha, Dhi, Vidya, Satya, and Akrodha—that guide life and leadership. This book unveiled the secrets of success, drawing inspiration from Narendra Modi's journey.

However, success is not the ultimate destination.

Success serves merely as a doorway to a deeper mystery. It reveals how the invisible powers within us—our willpower and our connection to the universe—can transform our lives.

Now, in "Dharma Path: The Secret Way to Manifestation " we venture into that unseen realm.

In this book, we will uncover not only theories but also the enigmatic principles that turn our desires into reality.

This journey will lead us to the universe within ourselves—a space where thoughts, willpower, and faith become vibrant forces that shape our existence.

If the first book clarified the essence of "success," then this second installment will unlock the door to its "secret."

Dharma path

the secret way to manifestation

Preface

Beginning of an Invisible Journey

Manifestation is not any "magic."

Many people associate it with magic or witchcraft, however the truth is, it is based on the science of the power and energy of the mind. We produce a vibration with our mind, and with our thoughts, and that vibration affects the world around us. That's why "as you think, you become" is not cliche but true.

Life as a human has always been a mysterious sojourn. Everybody wants to be successful, yet the road to success is usually draped with a mist. And that fog is not just of the external variety, but also of our inner hidden thoughts, resolutions, and beliefs.

Sanatan Dharma says –

"यथा मनोमयीं विश्वं यथाकल्पितमेव च।"

(Yoga Vasistha)

Insight This world in which you live and of which you are a part looks as it does because it's made from the thought

stuff of imagination and the resolve of our mind.What it means for all of us You live in a world that is both real and symbolic.

This is the first door of the secret that- our minds and our thoughts create our own world.

Sanatan Darsan – What is the Secret?

The Vedic rishis would say that the secret is not out there, it is hidden within.

We are already endowed with the power that we seek outside in our mind and soul.

The Upanishads teach us:

"अयं आत्मा ब्रह्म"

(This soul itself is Brahman.)

That is, we will if we glance inward at ourselves

find that our soul itself is that divine energy which is connected to the entire universe. This very energy decides our success, failure, and direction of life.

3. The First Sign of the Secret – Power of Thought

Picture yourself standing on the shore, with waves continuously rolling in and out. You can't stop them, but how you respond is entirely up to you. Similarly, waves of thoughts flow into our minds. By embracing positive thoughts, we move forward in life. Conversely, if we chase after negative thoughts, we either stall or regress.

The Rigveda states:

"मनसि जातं वचसि जातं कर्मणि जातं महद् भूतं भवति।"

(What is born in thought appears in speech and action, and that becomes the great outcome.)

4. The Second Sign of the Secret - Faith

Merely having thoughts is insufficient, as thoughts lacking faith are incomplete. Faith serves as an invisible bridge linking imagination to reality. Without faith, a resolution exists solely in the realm of imagination. However, when faith is present, that imagination gradually starts to take shape as reality.

5. The Third Sign of the Secret - Dharma and Success

Our lives are not just a series of personal desires. Success becomes truly meaningful and enduring when it aligns with Dharma.

"धर्मो रक्षति रक्षितः"

(The one who protects Dharma, Dharma protects him.)

When our actions are in harmony with Dharma, the universe itself starts to work in our favor.

6. The Secret Hidden in History

Throughout history, remarkable individuals have understood and utilized this secret.

In the Gita, Lord Shri Krishna taught Arjuna that "your battle is not external; it resides within your mind. Master your mind, and only then will victory be yours."

Swami Vivekananda stated, "We become what we think. Therefore, elevate your thoughts to be high, great, and divine."

Mahatma Gandhi transformed truth and non-violence from mere ideas into guiding principles of conduct. His steadfast inner resolve was powerful enough to challenge an empire.

In today's world, Narendra Modi Ji exemplifies this principle. A boy from a humble background who sold tea at a railway station rose to lead India through the strength of his thoughts, perseverance, and determination. This story reflects not just an external struggle but also a journey

towards uncovering the inner power we all possess.

7. Example - An Ordinary Man, Extraordinary Change

Imagine a farmer with a small plot of land. If he only thinks, "I hope my crop turns out well," the outcome is likely to be mediocre. However, if he resolves:

"I will work hard, serve the land with integrity, and respect nature."

This mindset transforms his thinking. He then dedicates himself fully—utilizing water, seeds, and fertilizer effectively. In this way, his determination aligns with the universe, leading him to achieve the success he envisioned.

8. Invitation to the Journey of the Secret

Dear reader, this book has found its way into your hands for a reason. This itself is a sign of that unseen force you are seeking, whether you refer to it as Prarabdha (destiny) or the Law of Attraction.

This journey will reveal:

- How to awaken the power of your thoughts

- How to strengthen your faith
- How to achieve success through the path of Dharma
- And how to uncover that hidden secret within you that can transform your life

From the Gita:

"श्रद्धावान् लभते ज्ञानम्"

(The one who has faith is the one who attains knowledge and success.)

Essence of the Introduction

The secret isn't magic; it's sadhana. This sadhana encourages us to align our mind, speech, and actions toward a single purpose. This book is your gateway to that secret. Now, you are not just meant to read it but also to embody its teachings.

Contents

Part I
Philosophy of Dharma & Manifestation

Chapter 1
Dharma and the Invisible Formula of Success

Introduction

"The path of Dharma aligns with cosmic power; those who follow it never lose their way."

Success isn't solely achieved through external effort or hard work. It stems from an invisible force, energy, and determination. In this chapter, we will explore how Dharma and cosmic law serve as the foundation for success in every aspect of our lives.

1. What is the Secret to Success?

Everyone desires success.

Some seek wealth, others crave respect, while some pursue knowledge or spiritual peace.

But why do certain individuals rise from ordinary circumstances to achieve extraordinary things, while others remain unfulfilled despite having all the resources?

The answer is simple: the invisible formula for success is "Dharma."

Dharma is not merely a matter of religious practice or worship. It represents the law, the natural order that governs the entire universe. Just as the sun rises and sets, rivers flow, and trees bear fruit, each person has their own Dharma.

When we adhere to that Dharma, success naturally follows us.

2. The True Meaning of Dharma

Dharma is often confined to the rituals performed in temples, mosques, and gurudwaras.

However, the Vedas and Upanishads offer a more profound understanding of Dharma.

Shloka (Manusmriti)

धरना धर्मं इत्याहुः धर्मो धार्यते प्रजा.

(Whatever sustains is Dharma; Dharma sustains people and society.)

In essence, Dharma is what nurtures life and maintains harmony within society and the universe.

Thus, Dharma encompasses duty, truth, justice, compassion, and balance.

3. The Hidden Formula for Success - Dharma and Attraction

This raises the question: how are Dharma and success connected?

If someone constructs their success solely on material resources, that foundation will be fleeting.

However, if their actions, thoughts, and goals are rooted in Dharma, that success becomes lasting and steadfast.

For example:

When a businessman operates according to Dharma, his enterprise thrives for generations.

When a leader makes decisions grounded in Dharma, the public places their trust in him for generations.

When a student dedicates himself to hard work in line with Dharma, his knowledge endures.

This is the unspoken formula for success.

4. Guidance from the Gita

In the Bhagavad Gita, Shri Krishna tells Arjun:

Shloka (Gita 2.47)

"कर्मण्येवाधिकारस्ते मा फलेषु कदाचन"

(You have the right only to perform your duty, never to the outcome.)

This verse uncovers the secret to success:

When we focus on our work according to Dharma without being preoccupied with results, those outcomes come naturally. However, when we fixate on the results, our efforts falter and success eludes us.

5. Story of Raja Harishchandra

A prime example of success rooted in truth and righteousness is Raja Harishchandra.

He sacrificed his kingdom, family, and comforts but never wavered in his commitment to truth and religion.

His life demonstrates that while the test of righteousness is challenging, it ultimately leads to enduring success.

Even today, people remember Raja Harishchandra, while many other kings from his era are forgotten.

This signifies that only success tied to righteousness is truly eternal.

6. Religion and Success in Modern Life

Today's society is so caught up in materialism that it equates money, status, and fame with success.

However, the reality is that success achieved solely through superficial means is incomplete.

A doctor who treats patients merely for financial gain

experiences only temporary success. In contrast, a doctor who views service and compassion as part of their duty enjoys genuine and lasting success.

Thus, religion serves as an invisible thread that not only brings success but also ensures its permanence.

7. Practicing the Awakening of the Invisible Thread

The question arises: how do we awaken this invisible thread in our lives?

Three essential steps are required:

Purifying thoughts - steering clear of negativity.

Aligning actions with Dharma - refraining from any behavior that harms others.

Setting high aims - focusing not just on personal gain but on the welfare of society and humanity.

The thoughts we entertain shape our mindset. If our thoughts are negative, our actions will reflect that negativity, leading to unfavorable outcomes. Conversely, if our actions align with Dharma and are positive, our aura will become strong, allowing us to envision greater objectives.

Shloka (Yajur Veda)

"सत्येनोत्तभिता भूमिः सूर्येणोत्तभितो द्यौः।"

(This earth rests on truth and the sky on the sun.)

In essence, truth and Dharma form the very foundations upon which the universe stands.

8. Essence - Dharma is the Seed of Success

Dear reader, if you seek genuine and lasting success in life, it must be rooted in Dharma.

Dharma is the seed from which the tree of success flourishes.

Without Dharma, success resembles a sandcastle—it crumbles at the first wave.

Only success grounded in Dharma brings meaning to your life; this is the hidden formula revealed within these pages.

Essence

The secret to success isn't solely hard work or luck.

It's a blend of hard work + faith + Dharma.

Understanding this formula is crucial for walking the path that leads to true, lasting, and divine success.

Chapter 2
Thoughts are the Seeds of Reality

Introduction

"You become what you think; your life reflects your thoughts."

People often blame their external circumstances, saying, "If only there were more opportunities, I would have succeeded."

However, the truth is that the foundations of success and failure lie within our thoughts.

1. The Mystery of the Seed and the Tree

Dear reader, have you ever observed how a tiny seed, when planted in the ground, can grow into a towering tree over time? The seed itself is invisible, and you cannot see the tree it will eventually become.

Yet that seed is the very essence of the future tree.

Similarly, our thoughts are the seeds of our future.

What you think today shapes your life tomorrow.

Shloka (Rig Veda)

"यद् भावं तद् भवति"

(A person becomes what they think.)

2. The Invisible Power of Thought

Though we can't see thoughts, their power is boundless.

Just like we cannot directly observe the flow of electricity, yet its effects are evident in bulbs, fans, and machines.

In the same way, while thoughts remain unseen, their outcomes are clearly reflected in our lives, personalities, and achievements.

- Positive thoughts lead to energy, confidence, and success.

- Negative thoughts result in fear, despair, and failure.

3. Perspective from the Upanishads

Shloka (Chandogya Upanishad)

"यथा मनसो ध्यायति, तद्भवति।"

(A person becomes what they think.)

4. Connection Between Thought and Action

Thoughts influence not only our mental state but also guide our actions.

Thoughts filled with fear and doubt lead to hesitant and unsuccessful efforts.

Conversely, thoughts rooted in faith and enthusiasm encourage courageous and successful endeavors.

Shloka:

"कर्मण्येवाधिकारस्ते मा फलेषु कदाचन।

मा कर्मफलहेतुर्भूर्मा ते सङ्गोऽस्त्वकर्मणि॥"

- Bhagavad Gita 2.47

(We have a right only to perform our duties, not to the outcomes.)

This highlights that the interplay between thoughts and actions is vital for success.

Ultimately, a person's character and fate are shaped not by external circumstances but by their own thinking.

5. A Story - Bricklayers

There were three laborers laying bricks.

When asked, "What are you doing?" the first one replied, "Can't you see? I'm laying bricks."

The second man said, "I'm building a wall."

The third one smiled and said, "I'm building a grand temple."

Though all three were engaged in the same task, their perspectives differed. This difference in thought influenced their energy, enthusiasm, and ultimately their results. It's essential to maintain purity and clarity in our thoughts.

6. From Thought to Destiny

What you think today shapes your actions tomorrow.

Your actions define your character, and your character determines your destiny.

Shloka (Mahabharata)

"मनः पूर्वं क्रियाणां हि सर्वाणाम्।"

(Before every action, a thought arises in the mind.)

Therefore, if your thoughts are pure, your actions will be pure as well; conversely, negative thoughts can lead actions astray.

7. Confirmation of Science

Modern psychology suggests that our thoughts influence our feelings and actions. If you repeatedly dwell on failure, your subconscious mind will steer you in that direction. Conversely, if you envision success, your subconscious will guide you toward achieving it.

Role of the Subconscious Mind

The subconscious mind is active around the clock, shaping our habits, decisions, and opportunities. When we focus on something consistently, the subconscious accepts it as "truth" and encourages us to pursue that path.

8. Practice – A Way to Change Thoughts

So, how can we cultivate positive thoughts?

Here are three simple methods:

Affirmations:

Start each morning by repeating positive statements – "I am capable, I am successful, the universe is supporting me."

Visualization:

Create a mental image of your success. If you aspire to be a doctor, picture yourself wearing a white coat. If you aim to be a businessman, envision yourself leading productive meetings in your office.

Company:

Our thoughts are influenced by our surroundings. Surround yourself with positive and inspiring individuals.

9. The Connection Between Dharma and Thought

Positive thinking alone isn't sufficient; it must align with Dharma.

When a person's thoughts are aimed at harming others, the outcome will inevitably be negative.

In contrast, thoughts rooted in Dharma, compassion, and truth resonate with the universe's energy and yield results more swiftly.

Shloka (Gita 17.3)

"सत्त्वानुरूपा सर्वस्य श्रद्धा भवति भारत।

श्रद्धामयोऽयं पुरुषो यो यच्छ्रद्धः स एव सः॥"

(As a person believes and thinks, so they become.)

10. A Modern Example

Thomas Edison - He faced thousands of failures before finally inventing the light bulb. Yet his mindset remained focused on one goal: "I have to make the bulb." Ultimately, he succeeded by having clarity in his vision, visualizing his dream, and consistently taking action.

Mahatma Gandhi – His entire movement was founded on the principles of "Non-violence and truth." This powerful idea brought down an empire.

Narendra Modi – A boy who sold tea never allowed his aspirations to shrink. Those same ambitions eventually led him to become the Prime Minister of India, realizing his dreams.

11. Conclusion – Thoughts are Seeds

Dear reader, your thoughts shape the future of your life.

Negative thoughts are like planting thorns.

Positive thoughts are akin to sowing fruitful trees.

Dharma-based thoughts resemble the Kalpavriksha.

Shloka (Atharvaveda)

"यच्चिन्तयति यद्भावयति तद्भवति।"

(Whatever a person thinks and meditates on becomes their reality.)

So, starting today, cultivate positive and uplifting thoughts aligned with Dharma.

This is your greatest asset in life.

Summary

Thoughts are the seeds from which the tree of reality grows.

If you aspire for success, ensure your thoughts align with both success and Dharma.

This insight will guide you toward true success.

Chapter 3
The Eternal Law of Attraction

Introduction

"As your attention goes, so does your world; as your belief shapes, so does your future."

Many people link success solely to hard work or luck. However, cosmic laws reveal that our thoughts, beliefs, and energy play a crucial role in shaping our reality.

This principle is known as The Eternal Law of Attraction.

"Everything you think and the energy you project draw similar experiences and opportunities into your life."

This law is supported by both scientific evidence and spiritual understanding.

From a scientific perspective: Every thought carries energy. This energy produces vibrations, and the universe responds accordingly.

On a spiritual level: Your mind and emotions resonate with the cosmic force.

Story:

A young woman was anxious about her business.

She often found herself thinking, "I will fail."

As a result of this negative mindset, new opportunities eluded her. However, when she shifted her thoughts to "I attract success," things began to change.

Gradually, the right people, opportunities, and situations started to enter her life.

Lesson: Energy and thoughts have a direct impact on life.

1. Mirror of the Universe

The universe reflects our thoughts and feelings.

When your mind is positive, compassionate, and enthusiastic, you attract positive situations.

Conversely, if your mind is filled with fear, doubt, and negativity, you'll encounter obstacles and failures.

Sutra 3:

"Whatever you attract inside manifests outside."

Story:

Every morning, a seeker would remind himself, "Today I will be a source of help and love for everyone."

That day, many people came to him for assistance, and he realized that his energy and aura drew people and circumstances his way.

2. Combination of Attraction and Faith

Attraction only works when combined with faith and belief. If you think, "I will succeed," but harbor doubts in your mind, the universe won't recognize that energy.

Proverb:

"Faith in truth and firm determination are the foundation of miracles."

Sloka:

"श्रद्धावान् लभते ज्ञानं तत्परः संयतेन्द्रियः।

ज्ञानं लब्ध्वा परां शान्तिमचिरेणाधिगच्छति॥"

- Bhagavad Gita 4.39

(He who is devoted and dedicated attains knowledge and power.)

This teaches us that energy transforms into reality not just through thought but also through faith and dedication.

3. Vibration of Energy

Every thought, emotion, and action creates vibrations that resonate with cosmic energy.

High vibrations—love, gratitude, enthusiasm—lead to positive experiences.

Low vibrations—fear, anger, negativity—result in obstacles and failure.

Story: An artist lived in anger each day. His efforts always fell short. However, when he infused love, gratitude, and hope into his mindset, his artwork began to gain recognition.

Lesson: The energy behind our thoughts and feelings forms the basis of attraction.

4. The Invisible Power of Attraction

Have you ever noticed how a magnet attracts iron?

Or how a sweet smell pulls us in its direction?

The same principle applies to our thoughts and feelings.

What we focus on repeatedly begins to come toward us.

This concept is known as the "Law of Attraction" in the Sanatan tradition.

Shloka (Rig Veda)

"यथा चिन्तयति मनः, तथैव भवति।"

(Life becomes what the mind thinks.)

5. The Eternal Law of Attraction

The Law of Attraction states:

"Whatever you focus on will grow in your life."

If you concentrate on success, love, peace, and prosperity, those elements will enter your life.

Conversely, if you dwell on fear, failure, and negativity, those will also be drawn to you.

This law transcends religion, caste, or nationality.

It is as universal as gravity.

Whether you believe it or not, it operates continuously.

6. View of Upanishad

Shloka (Mundaka Upanishad)

"यथा कर्म यथा श्रुतं च, यथा मतिः तद्भवति।"

(A person becomes what they act upon, think about, and believe.)

This clearly indicates that our lives are shaped not just by external circumstances but also by our power of attraction.

A story - The farmer and the seed

A farmer plants two seeds in his field.

The first seed represents "success."

The second seed symbolizes "fear and failure."

He waters the first seed daily and gives it his attention.

Meanwhile, he neglects the second seed.

In time, the first seed grows into a tree that bears fruit while the second one withers away and disappears.

This illustrates the law of attraction.

The thoughts you nurture most will manifest in your life.

7. Science and attraction

Modern science acknowledges that our thoughts emit energy.

Brain waves send energy outward as well.

When we contemplate something deeply, that same energy influences our surroundings.

That's why it's often said - "Focus on what you want to achieve, not on what you wish to avoid."

8. Message of the Gita

In the Bhagavad Gita, Lord Krishna tells Arjun -

Verse (Gita 6.5)

"उद्धरेदात्मनाऽऽत्मानं नात्मानमवसादयेत्।

आत्मैव ह्यात्मनो बन्धुरात्मैव रिपुरात्मनः॥"

(A person can elevate themselves through their thoughts or bring themselves down with the same.)

This reflects the law of attraction.

Your thoughts have the power to lift you to great heights or pull you into despair.

9. Negative Attraction – A Cautionary Note

The Law of Attraction operates in both positive and negative directions.

If you constantly think – "I will fail; people will mock me; I lack resources" – these beliefs may start to materialize in your life.

Shloka (Atharva Veda)

"यद्भावं तद्भवति।"

(Whatever you think is what happens.)

10. Practice – Method to Awaken the Law of Attraction

Now the question is: how can you harness this law to work in your favor?

Clarity of Intention:

Clearly define what you want.

Vague goals never attract positive outcomes.

Positive Visualization:

Spend some time each day visualizing your success.

For instance, picture yourself delivering a speech on stage or moving into your dream home.

Feel the Emotion:

It's crucial to genuinely experience the emotions that come with your success, not just think about it.

If you desire wealth, first embrace the feeling of being rich.

Righteous Purpose:

Your reasons for attracting should align with Dharma.

If they are solely based on selfish motives, the results will not be lasting.

11. Modern Examples

In 2014, Narendra Modi announced his candidacy in Varanasi, stating, “I have come to Kashi not to contest elections but to serve Ganga Maayya.” The universe responded, and people's hearts naturally gravitated toward him.

Steve Jobs viewed Apple not merely as a business but as a vision—a vision that drew the world's attention to technology.

Sachin Tendulkar nurtured a childhood belief that he was meant for cricket. That conviction attracted all the circumstances necessary for his success.

A.P.J. Abdul Kalam consistently envisioned India as a developed nation. This mindset not only made him an esteemed scientist but also earned him the titles of "Missile Man" and President of India.

12. Conclusion – The Secret of Attraction

Dear Reader, the Law of Attraction is not a recent concept; it has been in effect since ancient times.

What you think, you become.

What you focus on expands.

What you believe manifests in your life.

Shloka (Gita 17.3)

"सत्त्वानुरूपा सर्वस्य श्रद्धा भवति भारत।

श्रद्धामयोऽयं पुरुषो यो यच्छ्रद्धः स एव सः॥"

(Man is shaped by faith and trust; he becomes what he believes.)

Summary

The timeless Law of Attraction is simply this:

"The energy you project will return to you."

So starting today, think, speak, and act in ways that reflect what you wish to bring into your life.

Chapter 4
Faith – The Invisible Bridge

Introduction

"Faith is the invisible bridge that connects your thoughts to cosmic reality."

Faith is crucial for achieving success and transforming your life completely.

It's not simply about believing in your mind; it's a blend of faith and experience.

1. The Bridge that Connects Us

Picture a river with two banks.

Standing on one side, you wish to reach the other, but the river flows deep and fast.

You can only cross it if there's a sturdy bridge in place.

In life, our thoughts represent one bank, while success represents the other.

The only way to span this gap is through faith.

Faith serves as the invisible bridge that links our imagination to reality.

Shloka (Mahabharata)

"श्रद्धा हि परमं बलम्।"

(Faith is the greatest power of man.)

2. Definition of Faith

Faith goes beyond mere thought. It means being entirely convinced within yourself that what you desire will indeed come to pass.

It's like a farmer who sows seeds, fully aware that they will sprout, even while still buried beneath the soil.

3. Importance of Faith

Faith possesses the ability to turn the unseen into the seen.

Without faith, our efforts can falter and remain unfulfilled.

Faith grounds the mind and ensures a steady flow of energy.

It empowers us to persevere in spite of challenges.

Story:

A Sadhak was diligently working toward his goal but felt disheartened by his lack of progress.

His Guru advised him, "You must have faith in your efforts; the outcome lies with the universe."

Once he began to act with complete faith, he found that his efforts started yielding success.

4. The Combination of Faith and Action

Faith is more than just a mental sentiment; when paired with action and effort, it creates an invisible bridge.

Faith + Action in the right direction = Success

Doubt + Incomplete effort = Failure

Shloka:

"योगः कर्मसु कौशलम्॥"

- Bhagavad Gita 2.50

(Yoga means performing work with skill, faith, and consistency.)

This illustrates that combining faith and action provides direction in life.

5. Faith and Doubt

On our journey to success, we are accompanied by two companions:

Faith - which propels us forward

Doubt - which holds us back

When our minds are filled with faith, even obstacles transform into opportunities. Conversely, doubt can turn the easiest path into a struggle.

Shloka (Gita 4.40)

"अज्ञश्चाश्रद्दधानश्च संशयात्मा विनश्यति।

नायं लोकोऽस्ति न परो न सुखं संशयात्मनः॥"

(The one who lacks knowledge and faith ultimately perishes.)

6. Story - Two Travelers and the Bridge

Two travelers arrived at the riverbank.

The first exclaimed, "This bridge looks weak; I can't cross it."

He remained there.

The second replied, "This bridge will help me get across," and he stepped forward with confidence, reaching the other side

safely.

This highlights the contrast between faith and doubt.

Where doubt presents an obstacle, faith serves as the force that propels us ahead.

7. Why Is Faith an Invisible Bridge?

Empowering thoughts - Nothing changes solely through thought; faith energizes those thoughts.

Elimination of fear - When we believe, fear dissipates automatically.

Connection to cosmic energy - Faith links us to divine power that guides our actions.

Magnet for success - Faith acts as a magnet that draws opportunities and resources towards us.

8. The Relationship Between Religion and Faith

In Sanatan Dharma, faith is referred to as "Shraddha."

It encompasses not only belief in God but also unwavering trust in oneself, one's actions, and one's determination.

Shloka (Gita 17.3)

"सत्त्वानुरूपा सर्वस्य श्रद्धा भवति भारत।

श्रद्धामयोऽयम् पुरुषो यो यच्छ्रद्धः स एव सः।।"

(A person's faith aligns with their nature; they become what they believe.)

This suggests that our faith shapes our personality and destiny.

9. The Combination of Faith and Action

Faith is more than just a mental sentiment; when paired with action and effort, it creates an invisible bridge.

Faith + Action in the right direction = Success

Doubt + Incomplete effort = Failure

Shloka:

"योगः कर्मसु कौशलम्।।"

- Bhagavad Gita 2.50

(Yoga means performing work with skill, faith, and consistency.)

This illustrates that combining faith and action provides direction in life.

10. Faith and Doubt

On our journey to success, we are accompanied by two companions:

Faith - which propels us forward

Doubt - which holds us back

When our minds are filled with faith, even obstacles transform into opportunities. Conversely, doubt can turn the easiest path into a struggle.

Shloka (Gita 4.40)

"अज्ञश्चाश्रद्दधानश्च संशयात्मा विनश्यति।

नायं लोकोऽस्ति न परो न सुखं संशयात्मनः॥"

(The one who lacks knowledge and faith ultimately perishes.)

11. Story – Two Travelers and the Bridge

Two travelers arrived at the riverbank.

The first exclaimed, "This bridge looks weak; I can't cross it."

He remained there.

The second replied, "This bridge will help me get across," and he stepped forward with confidence, reaching the other side safely.

This highlights the contrast between faith and doubt.

Where doubt presents an obstacle, faith serves as the force that propels us ahead.

12. Why Is Faith an Invisible Bridge?

Empowering thoughts – Nothing changes solely through thought; faith energizes those thoughts.

Elimination of fear – When we believe, fear dissipates automatically.

Connection to cosmic energy - Faith links us to divine power that guides our actions.

Magnet for success - Faith acts as a magnet that draws opportunities and resources towards us.

13. The Relationship Between Religion and Faith

In Sanatan Dharma, faith is referred to as "Shraddha."

It encompasses not only belief in God but also unwavering trust in oneself, one's actions, and one's determination.

Shloka (Gita 17.3)

"सत्त्वानुरूपा सर्वस्य श्रद्धा भवति भारत।

श्रद्धामयोऽयं पुरुषो यो यच्छ्रद्धः स एव सः॥"

(A person's faith aligns with their nature; they become what they believe.)

This suggests that our faith shapes our personality and destiny.

Chapter 5
The Power of Imagination and Visualization

Introduction

"Whatever is clearly envisioned in the mind transforms into reality."

Imagination goes beyond mere mental play; it serves as the foundation of creation. A person who grasps the significance of imagination and visualization can steer the course of their own life.

1. Imagination: The Journey from Invisible to Visible

The most remarkable aspect of the human mind is its imagination.

This power has shaped our world from ancient times to the present day.

Airplanes, computers, the internet, magnificent temples,

scientific discoveries—everything first emerged as an idea in someone's mind.

Imagination is like a seed that contains the potential for future growth.

When we close our eyes and envision a goal or dream, it's not just a fleeting thought. It serves as a dialogue with the universe. Our imagination acts as a bridge that allows invisible energy to manifest in our real lives.

In Sanatan Dharma, it is believed that creation itself originated from "Imagination." Brahma first conceived creation in his mind before giving it form.

In this tradition, imagination is referred to as the creative power of the mind.

The sages have expressed this concept:

"यथा कल्पितं जगत् तिष्ठति, तथा कल्पनया सर्वं साध्यते।"

(Meaning: Just as this world exists through God's imagination, similarly everything is possible through human imagination.)

2. Imagination – The Creative Tool of the Universe

Imagination transcends simple thoughts; it is a divine gift bestowed upon humanity by God.

What you can vividly see in your mind can become part of your life.

The universe captures these mental images and orchestrates events accordingly.

If fear occupies your thoughts, then fearful experiences will manifest in your life. Conversely, if you focus on images of prosperity, success, love, and righteousness, those will also take shape in your reality.

3. Imagination from a Vedic Perspective

As stated in the Rig Veda:

"मनसा कल्पितानि विश्वानि कर्माणि।"

(All actions conceived in the mind take place in the world.)

Indian sages regarded 'Kalpana' not merely as dreaming but as true visualization.

In Yoga philosophy, this concept is known as Sankalpa Shakti.

When a practitioner visualizes their goals during meditation and sadhana, they harmonize their mind, prana, and cosmic energy toward a single purpose.

4. The Science of Imagination - The Power of the Mind

Modern science reveals that when we imagine something, our brain activates in much the same way as if that scenario were actually unfolding.

Athletes often use visualization techniques before practice, and research shows that this can significantly enhance their performance.

Doctors have observed through MRI scans that when a person visualizes success, health, or love, the body produces dopamine and other positive hormones, which can genuinely alter their condition.

Medical professionals indicate that patients who maintain a positive visualization of their health tend to recover more quickly.

5. Sanatan Dharma and the Tradition of Imagination

India's Rishi tradition stands as a remarkable example of imagination and meditation.

In the dialogue of Arjuna's Geeta: When Arjuna felt confused in battle, Lord Krishna reminded him with the words "Manasa Chintyate Vishwam," which means the world is created and experienced by the mind.

The penance of sages: They traveled to divine realms solely through meditation and imagination, without any physical exertion.

"सङ्कल्पमूलं कर्म, कल्पनासिद्धिर्भवति।"

(This translates to: Every action begins with determination and imagination; only what is vividly pictured in the mind comes to fruition.)

6. Real-Life Examples

A.P.J. Abdul Kalam once watched birds soaring in his childhood and envisioned India having its own airplanes. That vision helped him become known as the "Missile Man."

Modi ji didn't limit his view of India to its geographical boundaries; he imagined India emerging as a central hub for global politics, technology, energy, and culture. Today, India is on that path.

7. The Secret of Imagination - The Visualization Technique

Imagination and depiction go beyond mere thinking; they are a deliberate process.

There are two fundamental principles for successful imagination:

Clarity - Formulate a clear picture of what you desire in your mind.

A vague wish rarely comes to fruition.

Emotion - When you immerse yourself in the feeling of living

out that imagination, its energy sends a message to the universe.

Similar to how an artist first envisions a painting before transferring it onto canvas.

Define your goal: Start by determining what you want in life—wealth, health, relationships, or success.

Visualization: Spend at least 10 minutes each day with your eyes closed, visualizing your desired situation as if it is occurring right now.

Add emotion: Go beyond simple visualization; also immerse yourself in feelings of joy, happiness, and peace associated with it.

Considerate intent: Focus not only on personal gain but also on how achieving your goal will benefit society or your family.

"Faith: The universe is attuned to your vibrations - trust in this completely.

8. The Impact of Negative Visualization

Just as positive visualization can yield remarkable results, negative visualization can lead to destruction.

When someone consistently envisions failure, fear, or illness, that becomes their reality.

In the Ramayana, Kaikeyi continually pictured Bharat as a king and Rama as a hermit - ultimately, that's what came to pass.

Thus, visualizing wisely is essential for Dharma.

9. Obstacles and Their Solutions

Doubt: This is the greatest adversary.

Remedy: Utilize Vedic Shlokas and positive affirmations.

Negative Visualization: If you constantly envision failure, that's the outcome you'll face.

Remedy: Swiftly replace that negative image with a positive one.

Impatience: Many desire immediate results.

Remedy: Cultivate patience. Your visualization will materialize when the universe aligns.

10. Conclusion - From Visualization to Reality

Vigilance isn't an illusion; it's a divine creative force.

You are shaped by your thoughts.

You craft your life according to your vision.

योगयुक्तो विशुद्धात्मा विजितात्मा जितेन्द्रियः।

सर्वभूतात्मभूतात्मा कुर्वन्नपि न लिप्यते।। ५-७।।

- Bhagavad Gita 5.7

(Meaning: A yogic practitioner with a pure soul and mastery over their senses acts through imagination and action without being attached.)

Message:

Your imagination serves as the blueprint for your life. If you envision your journey toward greatness, service, and Dharma, the universe will surely guide you in that direction.

Imagination is more than mere play; it is a practice. When the mind, emotions, and faith unite to create an image, the entire universe begins to turn it into reality. Those who have mastered the art of imagination have discovered the key to shaping their future."

Part II
Practice of Energy & Mind

Chapter 6
Meditation – Awakening the Inner Energy

"Meditation is the key that unlocks the infinite power within you."

Meditation is more than just a path to mental peace; it's about aligning your body, mind, and energy. By awakening your inner energy through meditation, your thoughts, beliefs, and actions come into harmony.

1. The Mysterious Door of Meditation

The human mind resembles an ocean filled with ceaseless thoughts. Just as waves never fully settle, our minds continuously generate ideas. These thoughts shape our reality, but when the mind is scattered, it becomes difficult to direct one's energy effectively. Meditation serves as the mysterious key that awakens the dormant energy within and helps individuals stay focused on their goals and dharma.

The Rig Veda states:

"ऋतं् च सत्यं चभीद्धात तपैसोऽध्याजायत"

(Rig Veda 10.190.1)

This translates to: Truth and Rta (law) arise from Tapa (concentration and meditation).

This verse teaches us that the order of the universe, along with the essence of truth and Dharma, is found within meditation and Tapa.

2. What is Meditation?

Meditation isn't merely about sitting quietly with closed eyes; it's a dialogue between the soul and the universe. When we enter a meditative state, our inner restlessness subsides, allowing our energy to concentrate and flow toward our objectives.

In essence, meditation involves:

Focusing the mind on the present moment.

Dissolving negative thoughts.

Connecting with cosmic energy.

3. The Secret of Success and Meditation

Every great leader, seeker, or achiever has harnessed the power of meditation.

Lord Buddha attained enlightenment through this practice.

Swami Vivekananda referred to meditation as the science of the soul.

Mahatma Gandhi once said, "If I don't meditate, my day will be wasted."

Currently, India's Prime Minister Narendra Modi went to the

Himalayas to meditate and achieve his life goals.

Meditation provides us with inner strength, helping us maintain balance in challenging situations and make sound decisions.

4. Types of Meditation

Mantra meditation involves focusing the mind by repeatedly chanting a specific mantra, name, or word.

For example: Om Namah Shivaya or Om Shanti.

Prana meditation focuses on breathing. Deep observation of breath can awaken a sense of inner peace.

Dhyana Yoga is described by Lord Krishna in the Gita, where he explains that a yogi stabilizes their mind and unites with both their soul and the Supreme Soul.

Creative meditation encourages you to visualize your goals or desires while meditating on them, enhancing imagination and attraction power.

5. The Science of Meditation and Energy

Modern science supports the benefits of meditation:

Brain waves calm down.

Stress hormones such as cortisol decrease.

Positive energy sources like serotonin and dopamine increase.

Thus, meditation serves not only as a spiritual practice but also as a scientific tool for success.

6. A Simple Process for Meditation (10 Minutes a Day)

Find a quiet place.

Sit comfortably with your spine straight.

Close your eyes and take deep breaths.

Concentrate on your breathing because as long as you are alive, your breath will be with you—say "Om" as you inhale and experience "Shanti" as you exhale.

Gradually, your mind will begin to settle down.

Now visualize your goal as if it has already been achieved.

7. The Connection Between Meditation and Religion

Meditation serves not only as a tool for self-improvement but also as a fundamental aspect of religion. Without meditation,

one's mind can easily become ensnared by external distractions. It purifies the soul, helping individuals remain committed to their spiritual journey.

Bhagavad Gita (6.6)

आत्मैव ह्यात्मनो बन्धुरात्मैव रिपुरात्मनः॥

This means that a person is both their own friend and foe. When the mind is disciplined, it becomes an ally; when left unchecked, it turns into the greatest adversary.

Meditation provides the means to turn the mind into a friend.

8. An Inspiring Story

Once, a businessman from Japan faced devastating losses in his venture. In his despair, he contemplated suicide until a monk introduced him to meditation. The businessman began practicing daily, and gradually, his mind found tranquility, allowing new ideas to emerge and enabling him to revive his business. Later, he reflected:

"For me, meditation was not just a spiritual practice but a rebirth of my life."

9. The Hidden Secret of Successful Individuals

Today, many prominent entrepreneurs and leaders around the world, including Steve Jobs, Oprah Winfrey, and Narendra Modi, engage in meditation. Modi ji states:

"Meditation provides me with immense energy and focus. This is the fundamental secret behind my success."

10. Conclusion

Meditation is a sacred practice that awakens the latent energy within individuals and grounds them on their path to success. It goes beyond simply calming the mind; it reveals the secret of connecting with the universe. Those who meditate tap into their inner power and attract success while adhering to their spiritual beliefs.

Thoughts to Reflect On:

"Meditation is the lamp that lights up the soul's path even in darkness."

Chapter 7
The Magnetism of Positive Energy

Introduction: The Secret of Energy

"The energy you emit attracts your reality." Positive energy is more than just an emotion; it is a vital force in our lives. It stems from our thoughts, feelings, and actions, drawing in the right opportunities and experiences in accordance with

cosmic laws.

Every particle in the universe is made of energy. Everything we think, say, and do represents a form of energy. Just as sunlight sustains life on Earth, our thoughts and feelings shape our reality. This unseen energy functions like a magnet—positivity draws in positive outcomes, while negativity pulls in negative ones.

Sanatana Dharma states:

"यथा भावो तथा सिद्धिः"

(As you sow, so you reap.)

In this chapter, we will explore how positive energy can transform our lives and how this magnetic force leads us toward success, happiness, and a virtuous existence.

1. The Root of Positive Energy

The source of positive energy lies within us. It awakens when:

Our minds are pure and clear.

Our thoughts are optimistic and righteous.

Our actions benefit others.

The Rig Veda reminds us:

“संगच्छध्वं संवदध्वं सं वो मनांसि जानताम्।”

(ऋग्वेद 10.191.2)

(Walk together, speak together and let all minds be of one mind.)

This verse not only emphasizes unity but also teaches us that when we collectively focus on positivity, the universe responds by amplifying our energy.

2. The relationship between thought and energy

Every thought emits a vibration.

When we think with love, gratitude, and joy, our vibration is high and vibrant.

Conversely, when we dwell on fear, anger, or jealousy, our vibration sinks to a low and heavy state. This vibration influences the reality we attract in the universe.

We should always chant a mantra with the intention of promoting the well-being of all people. Regardless of whether you feel happy or sad, you should consistently chant:

“भवतु सब्ब मङ्गलम्”

This means "may everyone prosper!"

By wishing for everyone’s prosperity, you include yourself in that wish, and good things will come your way too. Your positive energy will resonate quickly with the universe, which

readily responds to such uplifting vibrations.

This is the power of positive energy.

3. Ways to awaken positive energy

Practice positive thinking -

In every situation, ask yourself, "what good can come from this?"

Mantra chanting and meditation -

Chanting "Om" helps purify both your mind and your surroundings. Since Om is the sound of the universe and represents the essence of nothingness, it carries profound significance.

Chanting Om Bhur Bhuvah Swaha elevates your vibrations.

Gratitude - Each morning, write down five things you are grateful for.

For instance: I am thankful for waking up this morning and being healthy.

I am grateful for my family, who supports me.

I appreciate nature for providing clean air and life.

I value my work/study opportunities that help me progress.

I am thankful for challenges that strengthen my resilience and patience.

Feel free to jot down new items each day or revisit those that hold special meaning for you.

Tip: As you write, don't just put down words; immerse yourself in the feeling of gratitude. This practice will have a transformative effect on your life.

Satsang and surrounding yourself with positive people - The company you choose influences the type of energy that connects with you.

Surrounding yourself with uplifting individuals -

These are people who bring enthusiasm to your life, inspire your growth, exhibit compassion and patience, and encourage the best within you rather than highlighting your weaknesses.

Daily practice:

Read an inspirational book for 10 to 15 minutes each day, whether it's the Gita, Upanishads, teachings of saints, or the biography of a remarkable individual.

Spend time with someone or a group of positive thinkers at least once a week.

Steer clear of negative discussions, such as gossip, anger, or criticism.

Surround yourself with people who are "energy givers" rather than "energy takers."

As stated in the Gita:

"सङ्गात् संजयते कामः।"

This means that the company you keep shapes your desires and nature.

4. The connection between positive energy and success

Successful individuals don't just work hard; they are filled with positive energy.

They turn setbacks into opportunities.

Their confidence inspires those around them.

Their presence draws others in.

The Upanishads remind us:

"उद्यमेऽहिं सिद्ध्यन्ति कार्याणि न मनोरथैः।"

(Work is achieved not merely through wishes but through positive efforts and energy.)

5. How to eliminate negative energy

Stop complaining.

Don't dwell on past mistakes.

Avoid the negative influences of television and social media.

Practice forgiveness.

Remember that forgiveness is the greatest source of positive energy.

6. Life Stories (Inspiration)

Swami Vivekananda famously said, "Arise, awake and stop not till you achieve your goal." His positive energy instilled self-confidence throughout India.

Mahatma Gandhi embodied immense patience and the spirit of non-violence. Though he lacked political power, his positive energy led to freedom for an entire nation.

Narendra Modi consistently highlights the importance of positive energy in his thoughts and lifestyle. He says:

-"Every difficulty is an opportunity."

-"Negative thinking offers no solutions; it only creates stress."

-"The strength of the country lies in the positive energy of its 1.4 billion citizens."

-"View criticism as an opportunity."

-"India's future is bright because of the vibrant energy of its youth."

7. Positive energy and the Law of Attraction

When you maintain a positive mindset and emotions, opportunities begin to present themselves.

You naturally attract the right people and situations into your life.

The universe reacts to your vibrations.

This is the essence of the Law of Attraction, which is also a principle found in Sanatan Dharma.

Positive energy combined with the Law of Attraction creates a pathway to success.

Positive thoughts lead to positive feelings, which inspire positive actions that result in positive outcomes.

Chapter 8
Negative Thinking: The Enemy of Success

Introduction – When the Mind Becomes an Obstacle

"Your greatest adversary is the doubt and negative thinking within you." We often point to external obstacles in life, but the truth is that our mental energy and mindset are at the core of our success or failure. Negative thinking casts a shadow over the light of your mind.

The primary enemy of our success lies not outside ourselves, but within – negative thinking.

This mindset gradually erodes our self-confidence, obscures opportunities, and disconnects us from the inherent power we possess.

As a religious perspective suggests – Conquer your mind, and you conquer the world; if your mind is defeated, everything else is lost.

Gita 6.5

"उद्धरेदात्मनाऽऽत्मानं नात्मानमवसादयेत्।

आत्मैव ह्यात्मनो बन्धुरात्मैव रिपुरात्मनः॥"

Meaning: One must uplift oneself rather than bring oneself

down—because one is both their own friend and their own enemy.

1) What is negative thinking?

Negative thinking refers to that mental tendency where—

we focus on dangers instead of possibilities,

we dwell on problems rather than seek solutions,

we give credence to fears and assumptions instead of facts.

It's more than just a "bad habit"; it's a drain on energy—patience, faith, motivation—all diminish.

2) Scriptural Warning: From Thought to Destruction

Bhagavad Gita 2.62–63 (the pitfalls of thought)

"ध्यायतो विश्यांपुंसः संगस्तेशूपजायते."

Sangat Sanjayate Kamah Kamat Krodho Bhijayate.

Krodhaad bhavati samohah samohaat smriti vibhramah।

Smriti Bhramshad Buddhinasho Buddhinashat Pranasyati.

Meaning: Negative rumination arises from attachments; desires lead to anger, anger breeds attachment, attachment results in loss of memory, and ultimately leads to the destruction of intelligence—which can cause downfall.

Message: As you think, so shall you be. Therefore, it's essential to halt negative thinking right at its source—in your thoughts.

3) What does science say?

Negativity Bias: The brain instinctively focuses more on negative signals (an old survival mechanism).

Amygdala Hijack: In moments of fear or anger, the nervous system triggers a "fight or flight" response; this hampers decision-making.

Cortisol Effects: Chronic exposure to stress hormones diminishes creativity, disrupts sleep, and weakens immunity.

Neuroplasticity: The good news is that the brain can change with practice; positive habits can strengthen new neural pathways.

4) Types of Negative Thinking (Identity Cards)

Catastrophizing: "Everything will go wrong!"

All-or-Nothing: "It's either perfect or worthless."

Mind Reading: "They're going to blame me."

Overgeneralization: "Once I lose, I'll always lose."

Labeling: "I am worthless."

Comparison Trap: "He's moving ahead—I'm falling behind."

Should/Must: "I must do this... or else I'm wrong."

Rumination: Fixating on the same thoughts repeatedly.

Recognizing these patterns is half the battle—once you identify them, it becomes easier to address.

5) Source: Where does negativity originate?

Inconsistency/Irreligion: Living in conflict with your core values.

Consistency and information-diet: Constant exposure to negative news or social media.

Sleep, diet, inactivity: A tired body leads to a tired mind and negative thoughts.

Unresolved experiences/traumas: Beliefs stemming from buried pain.

Unrealistic goals/perfectionism: Self-inflicted stress and pressure.

6) Effects: Energy, work, and relationships

Energy: Fatigue, procrastination, and indecisiveness.

Work: Missed opportunities, stifled creativity, and fear of taking risks.

Relationships: Irritability, distrust, and emotional distance.

Spirituality: Instability during chanting and meditation; a loss of faith.

Gita 17.28

"अश्रद्धया हुतं दत्तं तपस्तप्तं कृतं च यत्।

असदित्युच्यते पार्थ न च तत्प्रेत्य नो इह॥"

Meaning: Actions taken without faith or positive feelings yield no fruitful results.

7) Story - Deepak

Two wolves (symbolic story): One inner wolf embodies anger, fear, and jealousy; the other represents love, patience, and compassion. Which will win? The one you choose to nourish (through meditation and thoughts).

8) Breaking the Cycle of Negative Thinking (Techniques)

Trigger → Thought → Emotion → Behavior → Result → (Reinforces the same belief)

STOP–THINK–CHOOSE (60-second method):

Stop: Pause and take three deep breaths.

Think: "Is this a fact or an assumption?"

Choose: Decide on a Dharma-based solution for your next step.

9) Dharma and Karma-Vishwa (Dharma-based vision)

Negative thinking often leads to actions rooted in adharma—such as jealousy, deceit, or laziness—and brings about similar outcomes.

Dharma-based positive thoughts lead to pure actions that result in favorable outcomes—this reflects the bright side of the Karma cycle.

Kathopanishad (chariot analogy)

"आत्मानं रथिनं विद्धि शरीरं रथमे"

Meaning: The senses are like horses; the mind holds the reins. If the reins are loose, the chariot strays. Control yourself to reach your destination.

10) Immediate "SOS" Techniques (1-5 minutes)

Box Breathing 4–4–4–4: Inhale for 4 seconds, hold for 4, exhale for 4, then hold again for 4.

Nadi Shodhana (1-3 minutes): Balancing the energies in your body, fostering peace of mind.

Mantra-Anchor: Recite "Om ShantiH ShantiH ShantiH" or "Om Namah Shivay."

Grounding 5-4-3-2-1: Identify 5 things you can see… taste 1 thing to help you return to the present.

Change body position: Sit up straight and pull your shoulders back—this can instantly improve your mood.

11) Long-term Transformation (at the sanskar level)

Meditation (10-20 min/day): Helps purify both prana and mind.

Healthy diet and sleep: Aim for 7–8 hours of sleep with less processed food.

Digital-fast: Spend 30 minutes screen-free in the morning and evening.

Satsang/Swadhyaya: Read one page from the Geeta or Upanishads daily.

Service and Gratitude: Perform one act of kindness each day plus write down five things you're grateful for.

Boundaries: Keep a distance from toxic people and negative information.

Geeta 17.3

"श्रद्धामयोऽयं पुरुषो यो यच्छ्रद्धः स एव सः॥"

Meaning: Our beliefs shape who we are.

12) Cognitive Reframing

ABC Model:

A (Adversity): The challenge or event.

B (Belief): Your interpretation of it.

C (Consequence): The emotions and actions that follow.

☞ Change B → C changes as well.

Reframe these examples:

"I may fail" → "I will prepare more; every effort makes me stronger."

"Everyone will judge me" → "Some might, but most won't—I'll focus on adding value."

"I don't have the resources" → "I have enough to get started; everything else will follow."

13) Mantras, Shlokas, and Their Uses

"Om Namah Shivaya"—Helps mitigate fear and anger while promoting stability.

"Om Gan Ganpataye Namah"—For removing obstacles.

"Asato ma sadgamaya, tamaso ma jyotirgamaya" (Brihadaranyaka Upanishad)

Meaning: Guide us from falsehood to truth, from darkness to light.

"यद्भावं तद्भवति।"

(Atharvaveda-Sutraartha)—Our feelings determine our destiny.

Method: Chant 108 times in the morning/evening with your breath; set an intention before chanting—"I choose light and let go of negativity."

14) 21-Day "Negativity Detox" Plan

Week 1 – Recognize & Stabilize

Days 1–3: Keep a thought diary—record three negative thoughts each day and fact-check them.

Days 4–7: Practice box breathing and Nadi Shodhan for 10 minutes daily, along with a 30-minute screen-free morning.

Week 2 – Replace & Energize

Days 8–10: For every negative thought, come up with one positive reframe.

Days 11–14: Write down five things you are grateful for each day and perform one act of service; focus on Satvik food.

Week 3 – Stabilize & Expand

Days 15–18: Engage in 15 minutes of meditation followed by five minutes of visualization.

Days 19–21: Create an If–Then plan for challenging conversations or tasks:

"If procrastination arises, start with the five-minute rule."

On Day 21, review what triggers stood out the most and set micro goals for the next month.

15) Workbook (self-study & practice)

A. Self-Assessment (0–4 points, total 40)

I often imagine the worst possible outcome.

I judge myself harshly.

I tend to procrastinate… (10 statements)

0–10: Mild | 11–25: Moderate | 26–40: High – Detox plan is essential.

B. Trigger Tracker (daily):

Trigger | Thought | Feeling | Action | New Reframe | Next small step

C. Daily Sankalp (Affirmations):

"I make decisions based on facts, not fear."

"I choose solutions that align with Dharma."

"Every day, in every way, I am improving."

D. Forgiveness Letter:

Write a letter to someone you hold a grudge against, even if you don't intend to send it; then burn or store it for heart purification.

16) Environment by Design

Identify apps that trigger negativity – mute notifications or silence them.

Display motivational quotes or slokas on your wall or lock screen.

Implement a weekly "no-gossip" rule at home or within your team.

Create an Energy Corner: A designated space for a lamp, incense sticks, or mantra chanting.

17) Relationship Hygiene

Set clear boundaries around critical or mocking communication.

Attend Satsang once a week—participate in religious or inspirational gatherings.

Practice empathy: Instead of reacting to others' negativity, respond calmly and kindly.

18) Managing Negativity at Work

Take two minutes of collective breathing or silence before meetings.

Use a "Problem-Solution-Next Step" template to minimize distractions.

Focus on pro-mortem strategies rather than post-mortem analysis for risk mitigation ahead of time.

Maintain a success log where the team shares three small wins weekly.

19) Closure—From Darkness to Light

Negative thinking should not be viewed as punishment; it is simply a signal that indicates it's time to change direction.

As Dharma suggests: Vichar ka havan—by sacrificing negativity, ignite the fire of positive resolution. Whenever doubt creeps in, remember—

Brihadaranyaka Upanishad

“असतो मा सद्गमय।

तमसो मा ज्योतिर्गमय।

मृत्योर्मा अमृतं गमय॥”

This translates to: Lead from falsehood to truth, from darkness to light, from death to immortality.

20) Takeaways

Recognize: Identify the negative thought by name.

Stop—Think—Choose: Shift direction within 60 seconds.

Breath—Mantra—Meditation: Reset your nervous system.

Gratitude—Service—Satsang: Purify both your heart and environment.

Reframe—Routine—Detox: Build new pathways in your brain.

Today's Sankalp: "I break the shackles of negative thinking and choose positive thoughts in accordance with Dharma. My mind is my friend—and I am the creator of my own light."

Chapter 9
The Mystery of Karma and Destiny

The Invisible Equation of Life

Introduction

"Work done in accordance with Dharma is the seed of lasting success and peace in life." Dharma encompasses more than just religious practices; it represents a path of truth, morality, justice, and service. Engaging in work that aligns with Dharma not only brings happiness to an individual but also positively influences society and the universe.

1. Unique Balance of Life

Karma and Destiny are two concepts that have long intrigued humanity. Many people believe that every event is predetermined, leading them to feel that their efforts are

pointless. Conversely, others hold the view that hard work alone guarantees success. However, the Sanatan perspective suggests that the truth lies somewhere in between.

Destiny sets the stage for our lives, while Karma shapes our performance on it. Just as we can plant a seed but rely on nature for rain to help it grow, so too are Karma and Destiny intertwined.

2. Guidance from the Gita - The Subtle Secret of Karma

Sri Krishna imparted this wisdom to Arjuna:

"Karmanyewadhikaraste ma phaleshu kadachana." (Gita 2.47)

This translates to saying that one has rights only over their efforts, not over the outcomes. Results emerge based on time, circumstances, and destiny.

In the fourth chapter of the Gita, Krishna notes that even the wise find it challenging to discern what constitutes karma versus akarma. Hence, liberation from negativity comes only through knowledge.

3. Destiny - The Invisible Stream

Destiny refers to the current shaped by our past actions and present situations, presenting us with both opportunities and

challenges.

Think of destiny like a flowing river; Karma is the boat we use to navigate it. By rowing our boat effectively, we determine our course. If we cease our efforts, however, we risk being carried away uncontrollably by the current.

Thus, a balanced life is attainable only when respect for destiny aligns with diligent effort through Karma.

4. Harmony of Karma and Destiny

Destiny offers us opportunities—such as mentors, guidance, or favorable situations—at critical moments. In turn, Karma allows us to seize these opportunities through hard work, courage, and patience. Ultimately, outcomes unfold according to destiny—sometimes swiftly and sometimes slowly.

For example: Shri Ram's exile was part of his destiny; however, his righteous behavior and restraint during this time were his actions (Karma). These actions ultimately led him to victory and honor.

5. The Science of Karma - From Seed to Tree

As the seed is sown, so shall the fruit be.

Good karma leads to positive results.

Inauspicious karma results in unhappy outcomes.

This principle is an unchanging law of the universe. Our fate is shaped solely by our karmas.

Sutra:

"Karma is the root of destiny, and destiny is its fruitful manifestation."

6. Three Dimensions of Karma

Accumulated karma - the total collection of past lives' actions.

Prarabdha Karma - That portion of accumulated karma which manifests in this present life.

Kriyaman Karma - The actions being taken today that will influence future circumstances.

This illustrates that destiny is not a predetermined path but rather a dynamic outcome. When current karma is aligned with goodness, destiny gradually shifts toward more favorable outcomes.

7. Negative Thinking vs. Karma-Niyati

Believing that "everything in my life is fixed and I can't change anything" reflects a mindset of complacency.

Destiny presents challenges, while karma empowers us to overcome them.

Destiny sets the stage, and karma determines whether we turn it into an opportunity or a failure.

8. Motivational Story - The Life of Karna

Karna was born into challenging circumstances—this was his fate. Yet, through his courageous actions, he became a renowned warrior in the Mahabharata. Ultimately, his negative karma led to his downfall, while his good deeds granted him immortality. This exemplifies the intricate balance of karma-niyati.

9. Modern Perspective - Thought and Energy

Modern science also acknowledges that:

Thought = Energy

Action = Direction

When thoughts and actions align harmoniously, destiny tends to support us.

For instance: If a student aspires to become an officer, success becomes achievable only through diligent study, discipline, and hard work infused with positivity.

10. Purity of Action - Service and Gratitude

Sanatan philosophy teaches that we should not act solely out of self-interest. When our work is tied to service, charity, and social welfare, it becomes pure, and destiny rewards us.

"श्रेयान् स्वधर्मो विगुणः परधर्मात्स्वनुष्ठितात्।

स्वधर्मे निधनं श्रेयः परधर्मो भयावहः॥"

(Gita 3.35)

It is better to fulfill one's own duties, even with imperfections, than to take on the responsibilities of others.

11. Conclusion - Destiny is the Beginning, Action is the Result

Destiny shapes our circumstances.

Karma transforms these circumstances into opportunities or challenges.

With righteous actions, destiny paves the way for success.

Sutra:

"Destiny is the stage; karma is its performance. One will reap results according to their actions."

12. Good Thoughts and Messages

"Destiny opens the door to opportunity; karma paves the path to success."

"Karma is the seed; destiny is the soil, and life is its tree."

"Do not shy away from destiny; reshape it through your actions."

When a person grasps the connection between karma and destiny, they truly understand the essence of life. While destiny sets limits, karma empowers us to transcend them.

True strength lies in accepting destiny and guiding it positively through good deeds.

Chapter 10
Righteous Actions and Their Consequences

1. The Secret of Karma

Karma serves as the foundation of human existence.

Regardless of a person's knowledge, if they fail to engage in work, they lose their connection to the rhythm of life. Lord Krishna clearly states in the Geeta:

"न हि कश्चित्क्षणमपि जातु तिष्ठत्यकर्मकृत्।

कार्यते ह्यवशः कर्म सर्वः प्रकृतिजैर्गुणैः॥"p

(Geeta 3.5)

This means that no one can remain inactive for even a moment; it is the qualities of nature that drive us to act.

But the pressing question is –

Is merely performing work sufficient?

Or is it the righteous nature of our actions that holds the true secret?

2. Righteous Actions Versus Irreligious Actions

In the pursuit of success, many people chase after results without considering whether their actions are right or wrong.

Unrighteous deeds may provide immediate rewards, but their outcomes are often fleeting and painful.

Righteous deeds might sometimes appear challenging, yet their results are lasting, pure, and fulfilling to the soul.

For example:

Ravana gained incredible power through his penance, but his actions were not aligned with Dharma, leading to his tragic downfall.

Conversely, Shri Ram opted for a more difficult path but engaged in dharmik actions. His reward was fame, dignity, and timeless ideals.

3. The Invisible Equation of Karma and Results

Every action we take is like a seed. Though small at first, when nurtured, it can yield significant results. This is reflected in scripture:

"यथा बीजं तथा फलम्।"

Meaning—The fruit you bear corresponds to the seed you plant.

In modern terms—

Our actions set into motion unseen vibrations throughout the universe. The universe keeps a record of every deed and delivers results accordingly.

4. The Coordination of Karma and Destiny

Many people say, "Everything is predestined."

However, the Gita teaches us that destiny can be altered through our karma.

For instance:

Consider Narendra Modi ji's journey from being a humble tea seller to becoming Prime Minister. If he had merely accepted

his circumstances as fate, such an achievement would have been impossible. He undertook Dharma-compliant actions—serving others with dedication and prioritizing national interests—and as a result, destiny favored him too.

5. Identification of Dharma-compliant deeds

What is the identification of Dharma-compliant deeds?

Selflessness - doing it above personal interest.

Society and national interest - which benefits others.

Scriptural path - which matches the values of scriptures.

Work related to truth and compassion.

If any deed benefits only you, but causes harm to others, then it is not Dharma-compliant.

6. Dharma Sammat Phal - The Real Definition of Success

The fruit of Dharma Sammat Karma is not just material success. It is achieved at three levels:

Material fruit - position, prestige, wealth.

Mental fruit - peace, self-satisfaction.

Spiritual fruit – progress towards salvation.

Examples:

Material success: Respect in society.

Mental success: Peaceful sleep at night.

Spiritual success: The feeling that you have fulfilled your duty.

7. Stories and Inspirational Episodes

a) Yudhishthira of Mahabharata

   Yudhishthira was Dharmaraj. After the war, he got the kingdom, but he never thought that only the result is important. He always considered Dharma Sammat Karma as supreme. That is why he was called "Dharmaraj".

b) Mahatma Gandhi

   Gandhiji also showed the same. He did not have weapons, but his actions were based on Dharma. As a result, he shook the whole empire. That is why he is called the Father of the Nation

8. Exercise for the Reader

Exercise for this chapter:

Every night before going to sleep, write down what Dharma-compliant deed you did today.

Ask yourself – "Did my today's deed benefit only me or the society as well?"

Perform one act of selfless service every week. (Like feeding a poor person, educating someone, helping someone.)

9. Good thoughts and sutras

"Karma is the Dharma of life."

"The fruit of Dharma-compliant deed is eternal, the fruit of Adharma is temporary."

"True success is that which satisfies the soul."

10. Conclusion - Connection to the first chapter

We saw in Chapter 1 that to open the door to the mystery, we have to understand the invisible powers.

Now Chapster 10 teaches us that the real secret of these invisible powers is hidden in Karma and its Dharma-compliant fruit.

If you do Dharma-compliant deed, the whole universe will work in your favour. This is the secret of success.

Part III
Values & Virtues

Chapter 11
The Miracle of Gratitude

One of life's simplest yet most profound secrets is gratitude.

Gratitude is not merely an emotion; it is a powerful force.

This power transforms your thoughts, purifies your actions, and creates an invisible aura around you.

When you express thanks, you convey to the universe that you accept, are satisfied, and are ready for more.

Sanatana Dharma has always emphasized that gratitude is a gateway to divinity.

That's why the Vedas and Upanishads refer to various "debts" - Dev Rin, Rishi Rin, Pitra Rin, and Matrubhumi Rin.

Life is a journey toward repaying these debts, with gratitude being the most significant way to do so.

Spiritual Foundation of Gratitude:

The Bhagavad Gita states:

"यज्ञशिष्टाशिनः सन्तो मुच्यन्ते सर्वकिल्बिषैः।

भुञ्जते ते त्वघं पापा ये पचन्त्यात्मकारणात्॥"

(Gita 3.13)

This means that those who offer their wealth to God with gratitude and enjoy the rest are freed from sin.

Conversely, those who live solely for themselves remain indebted and unhappy.

This verse clearly illustrates that gratitude embodies not just morality but also the path to spiritual liberation.

The Secret of Gratitude in Life and Success

The Flow of Energy -

Gratitude is more than just saying thank you—it is a powerful force that transforms your inner world. The moment you express genuine thanks, you release the weight of negativity, stress, and resistance that may be clouding your mind. That heavy energy dissolves, creating space for lightness, clarity, and positivity to enter.

When your heart is filled with gratitude, your energy begins to flow in harmony with the universe. You become like a magnet, radiating positivity, and in turn, life reflects that

same energy back to you. Opportunities open, relationships deepen, and even challenges start to feel like stepping stones rather than obstacles.

Gratitude shifts your vibration to one of abundance. Instead of focusing on what is missing, you begin to notice the blessings already around you. This heightened awareness fuels your success because the energy you send out—joy, appreciation, and optimism—returns to you multiplied.

In essence, gratitude is not just a practice; it is a gateway to aligning with the infinite flow of universal energy, where peace, prosperity, and fulfillment naturally flourish.

The Foundation of Manifestation -

Manifestation is like planting seeds in the garden of the universe. But those seeds cannot bloom without the nourishing water of gratitude. When you overlook the blessings already present in your life, you send a message of lack, as if what you have is not enough. And if the universe senses ingratitude, why would it pour more abundance into hands that do not value it?

Gratitude, however, transforms everything. The moment you give thanks—even for the smallest blessing—you ignite a spark of magic. That spark grows into a radiant light, signaling to the universe that you are ready, worthy, and open to receive more.

Think of gratitude as a key that unlocks hidden doors. With every heartfelt thank you, the universe whispers back, "Here is more for you, because you truly see, value, and cherish what already flows your way."

Without gratitude, manifestation is like a spell half-cast, an intention without wings. But with gratitude, your desires take flight, carried by the energy of appreciation into the boundless field of possibilities—where abundance multiplies and miracles unfold.

Contentment and Joy -

Gratitude is a gentle shield that protects your heart from the poison of comparison and envy. The moment you choose to celebrate what you already have, you step out of the endless chase of measuring yourself against others. Instead of longing for someone else's path, you find peace and delight in your own journey.

True joy is born not from accumulation, but from appreciation. When you can look at your life and smile at its blessings—big or small—you rise above jealousy and discontent. This inner contentment becomes your strength, and from that steady foundation, you gain the freedom and clarity to climb toward even greater heights.

Inspirational Incidents:

1. **Narendra Modi**

   Upon taking office as Prime Minister, he expressed his gratitude to his village, his mother, and his teachers. In every address, you may have noticed that Modi ji consistently acknowledges the people of the country, along with workers and colleagues. This sense of gratitude has fostered a strong bond between him and the public. He stated, "Whatever I am, it is the blessing of Mother India and her children."

2. **The Story of a Sadhak**

   A young sadhak from Varanasi practiced gratitude each day: "Thank you for the food I received today. Thank you for the breath I took today. Thank you for the chance to learn today."

In just a few years, his life was filled with miracles—financial success, spiritual growth, and social recognition.

Practice: The Practice of Gratitude

Dedicate 5-10 minutes every morning and evening to "Thank You Writing."

What are ten things you are grateful for today?

Who inspired you today?

What opportunity enriched your life today?

Keep a gratitude diary. On each page, write:

"I am grateful because..."

Pray:

"O God, I thank You for every gift, big or small."

Dharma-Compliant Gratitude:

Sanatan Dharma speaks of four debts:

1. Dev Rin - Gratitude towards the Sun, Moon, Air, Fire, and Water.
2. Rishi Rin - Gratitude towards the knowledge tradition of the Vedas, Gita, and Upanishads.
3. Pitru Rin - Gratitude towards one's ancestors and parents.
4. Manav Rin - Gratitude towards society, nation, and humanity.

When a person acknowledges these debts and expresses thanks, their life aligns with Dharma.

The Secret of Gratitude and Success

A grateful person remains humble and is cherished by others.

Society places trust in such individuals.

Trust forms the foundation of success.

An essential truth is that the more one expresses gratitude, the more returns to them.

This is an unchanging law of the universe.

Inspirational Quotes:

"Gratitude turns even sorrow into opportunity."

"There is no limit to what one can achieve if they know how to say thank you."

"Gratitude is the greatest gateway to prosperity."

Conclusion:

Gratitude is not a minor emotion; it holds the deepest secret to success.

It is rooted in religion; it represents spiritual practice and elevates life to a divine level.

A person who gives thanks for their life each day will never feel empty.

"न तस्य कृतेनार्थो नाकृतेनेह कश्चन।

न चास्य सर्वभूतेषु कश्चिदर्थव्यपाश्रयः॥"

(Gita 3.18)

Meaning: A grateful and self-satisfied individual harbors no selfishness in any action they take. They become a source of joy and success.

Chapter 12

Invisible Success through Service

Introduction

"Service is the invisible path that brings happiness, peace, and success in life."

Service goes beyond merely doing things for others; it's an extension of our mind, energy, and soul. When we serve selflessly, the universe responds by bringing us positive experiences and opportunities.

1. The Secret of Service

As we continue on the journey along the path of Dharma, we now arrive at a chapter where the greatest hidden secret to success lies—Selfless Service (Seva).

Sanatana Dharma repeatedly teaches us that true success is not solely about personal accomplishments; rather, illuminating the lives of others represents the highest purpose in life.

The secret to success is that when you do good for others, the universe works in your favor with amplified energy.

"यथा ददाति तथा लभते।"

- As you give, so you receive.

2. Viewpoint of Scriptures

In the Bhagavad Gita (3.10), Shri Krishna addresses Arjuna:

"Sahyajnaah prajaah srishtva purovacha prajapatih.

Anena prasamishyadhvamesha vo'astvishtakamadhuk.."

This means that while creating the world, Brahma fashioned humans with yajna (service and sacrifice) and declared that through yajna (selfless work), you will attain prosperity and fulfill all your desires.

Here, "yajna" refers not only to rituals or ceremonies but also encompasses selfless service and sacrifice.

3. The Invisible Bond of Service and Success

Service is the unseen seed that carries within it the entire blueprint of success. When you plant this seed through acts of selflessness, it takes root in the unseen realms and grows into a mighty, invisible tree whose fruits are prosperity, peace, and fulfillment.

Every act of true service gently dissolves the grip of the ego. The "I, me, mine" begins to fade, and in its place arises a deeper connection with the vastness of life. As the ego melts away, the doors of the universe open, and cosmic energy begins to flow freely into one's existence.

This divine current carries with it opportunities, abundance, and inner harmony—things that cannot be forced or chased, but which arrive naturally when the heart is aligned with service. Just as rivers flow effortlessly toward the ocean, so too does success flow toward those who give of themselves without expectation.

Look at the great souls who have walked this earth—saints, visionaries, leaders, and creators. Their legacy was not built by seeking glory for themselves, but by dedicating their lives to the upliftment of others. Service was their foundation, and success became an inevitable companion.

In truth, service is not just an act—it is the alchemy that transforms ordinary lives into extraordinary journeys, weaving an invisible bond between giving and receiving, between humility and greatness, between humanity and the divine.

4. Example from life

Swami Vivekananda said: "The more you can serve others, the more power will manifest within you."

He dedicated his life to the service and awakening of Mother India and today he is immortal.

Mahatma Gandhi - He did not do politics of power, but considered "service" as his religion. As a result, he alone, being a resourceless person, was able to shake the entire empire.

Narendra Modi - His whole life started with service. Following the principle of "service is organization", he made politics a medium of service. Modi ji says that I am not the Prime Minister but the Prime Servant. This is the reason why his success became not just a personal achievement, but the faith of crores of people.

5. Types of service

Physical service - helping someone, supporting the needy.

Economic service - Giving money, clothes, food or resources.

Intellectual service - Giving knowledge, education and inspiration.

Spiritual service - Showing others the path of religion, meditation and peace.

Every service has its own importance, and every service

invisibly sows the seeds of success for you in the universe.

6. Effect of service towards success

Service gives you three invisible blessings:

Blessings - When a needy person smiles because of you, the blessings of his soul illuminate your life at that moment.

Karma purification - Service lightens the burden of your bad karma and accumulates good karma.

Cosmic attraction - A person doing service automatically becomes a magnet of positive energy.

7. Modern Context

In today's fast-paced and competitive world, the idea of service is often misunderstood as something limited to charity or large-scale humanitarian work. But true service is far more expansive, subtle, and deeply woven into the fabric of our daily lives.

Every small act of kindness carries the essence of service. Offering a word of encouragement to someone who has lost faith in themselves can become the spark that reignites their journey. Believing in another person's dreams, even when the world doubts them, is a profound service, because you are lending them strength, hope, and courage when they need it most.

Service also takes root in the quiet sacrifices we make for our loved ones. Providing for your family, giving up comfort for their well-being, or simply being present in times of need—these too are forms of service, though they may never be publicly recognized.

Each of these seemingly small actions is a seed planted in the soil of life. Over time, these seeds grow into towering trees, bearing fruits of success, harmony, and fulfillment—not only for the one who serves but also for those touched by their kindness. In this way, modern service becomes a silent yet powerful force that shapes lives, uplifts communities, and creates a ripple of abundance that spreads far and wide

8. Quotes

"Service is the true sadhana."

"The one who gives receives."

"The one who serves never fails."

"The one who lifts others rises himself."

9. Conclusion - From Service to Success

Success isn't about magic; it's a law rooted in Dharma.

When you serve, you align yourself with the universe's laws.

And when you're aligned, the rhythm of life naturally elevates you to new heights.

So as you walk along the path of Dharma, remember:

"Service is the invisible secret of success."

This is the bridge that connects the insights we've gathered from Chapter 1 to present reality.

Chapter 13
The Secret of Patience and Consistency

Introduction: "Patience is the most powerful weapon that leads to success over time and through various circumstances."

Patience and consistency serve as the two essential pillars of life.

Often, we embark on a new endeavor only to feel disheartened when immediate results don't materialize.

True success is attained by those who possess the patience to endure the test of time and persistently keep trying.

Patience - The Quiet Seeker of Success

The journey to success is never a sudden leap; it unfolds gradually, much like a flower blossoming. Just as a seed doesn't sprout immediately upon being planted, your dreams and efforts also require time, nurturing, and faith to come to life. The path is filled with twists, setbacks, victories, and long stretches of waiting. In this intricate dance, one quality serves as the anchor that holds everything together—patience, accompanied by consistency.

Patience embodies a quiet trust in life's timing. It's the wisdom to understand that rushing won't speed up growth and that every stage of struggle is secretly preparing you for what lies ahead. It's the ability to remain calm when results seem delayed, to persevere when others give up, and to keep believing even when the outcomes of your labor are not yet visible.

Consistency is patience put into action. It reflects the steady rhythm of showing up day after day and taking one step forward, no matter how small. Success rarely comes from giant leaps; instead, it's the result of countless small actions repeated over time. Consistency turns discipline into progress, and progress into achievement.

Together, patience and consistency create an invisible partnership. Patience grants you the faith to wait without frustration, while consistency ensures that you continue moving forward during that wait. Each one alone is incomplete—patience without action leads to stagnation, while action without patience results in burnout.

Every remarkable success story is built on these two virtues. Whether it's an artist honing their craft, an entrepreneur realizing their vision, or a student striving for mastery—patience and consistency quietly work behind the scenes, transforming effort into excellence and dreams into reality.

Patience - The Quiet Seed of Success

Patience means remaining untroubled even when life doesn't yield immediate results.

Consider a farmer who plants seeds and waters them. He understands that it will take time for those seeds to sprout and bear fruit.

In much the same way, when we plant the seeds of our thoughts and resolutions, they also require time and practice to grow.

Without patience, a person remains unfinished.

For instance –

If Arjuna had lost his patience on the battlefield, the dialogue in the Gita would never have taken place.

"If Mahatma Gandhi had lost patience during Satyagraha, the freedom struggle would have remained unfinished.

If Narendra Modi had been impatient in the early days of his journey, he wouldn't have reached the position of Prime Minister.

Continuity - The great strength of small steps

Continuity is the force that turns the ordinary into the extraordinary.

When each drop of water falls consistently, it can even penetrate the hardest stone.

Daily yoga practice transforms both body and mind.

If a student studies consistently, they can evolve from ordinary to extraordinary.

"Success does not happen overnight; it is the result of many small, ongoing efforts."

The balance of patience and continuity

Only having patience can lead to laziness, while solely relying on continuity can foster impatience.

The ideal approach is to find a balance between patience and continuity.

Patience reminds us: "Results will take time."

Continuity encourages us: "Keep trying every day."

Together, these elements create miracles.

Story: A sculptor and his statue

A renowned sculptor worked on a stone every day. For years, he hammered away at it without any visible results. People often mocked him.

But one day, out of nowhere, the stone cracked open and revealed a magnificent statue inside.

People exclaimed - "This happened with just one blow."

The sculptor smiled - "No, that was not just one blow; it was the culmination of thousands of persistent strikes."

This illustrates the secret behind patience and continuity.

Eternal Perspective

The Upanishads state:

"श्रद्धावान् लभते ज्ञानं तत्परः संयतेन्द्रियः।

ज्ञानं लब्ध्वा परां शान्तिमचिरेणाधिगच्छति॥"

This means that only a person who possesses faith, patience, and self-control attains knowledge and success.

This highlights that patience and continuity are vital for achieving success along spiritual paths.

Benefits of patience and continuity

Peace of mind - Impatience brings stress; patience calms the mind.

Self-confidence - Continuous effort boosts self-assurance.

Ability to make sound decisions - A patient individual can make wise choices even in challenging situations.

Attraction power - The universe tends to support those who remain steadfast in their commitments.

Example of Narendra Modi

Narendra Modi's life exemplifies patience and consistency beautifully. As a young man from humble beginnings, he dedicated years as a Sangh worker without seeking recognition. His life prior to becoming Chief Minister was

filled with challenges and waiting but he didn't give up.

Chapter 14
The Light of Inspiration and Self-Confidence

Introduction

"Inspiration is the fire that burns within, while self-confidence is the light that guides our path."

Both motivation and self-confidence are vital for achieving success and maintaining balance in life. These qualities empower us to move forward even in challenging times. Inspiration ignites our ambitions, while self-confidence reassures us of our strength and capabilities.

1. Beginning - The Light Within

The key to success lies not solely in external factors but in the inner light of inspiration and self-confidence that awakens from within.

When someone embarks on a significant goal, the first voice

they hear is one that comes from within: "You can do it."

This voice represents inspiration. As we begin to trust this voice more and more, it transforms into self-confidence.

Sanatan Dharma teaches us:

"Uddhredaatmanaatmanam naatmanamvasaadayet."

(Bhagavad Gita 6.5)

This means: One should uplift oneself rather than bring oneself down.

This verse encapsulates the essence of motivation and self-confidence—believe in yourself, for only then can you inspire others.

2. Motivation - The Invisible Spark

Motivation isn't something external; it's a fire that resides within us. Just as a spark is necessary to ignite dry wood, a spark of motivation is essential for moving toward success.

Motivation provides us with reasons to rise.

It stirs enthusiasm within us.

It guides us along paths that remain joyful despite their challenges.

When Swami Vivekananda spoke in Chicago, his confidence and powerful address stemmed not just from knowledge but from deep inspiration. He didn't merely deliver words; he conveyed an energy that resonated with everyone present.

3. Self-Confidence - The Backbone of Success

While motivation sets us in motion, self-confidence ensures we complete the journey.

Self-confidence acts as the golden thread linking our dreams to reality.

When our self-confidence is strong, failures become valuable lessons rather than roadblocks.

Sanatana Dharma reminds us:

"Na hi kalyana kritka ashchiddurgatim tat gacchati."

(Bhagavad Gita 6.40)

This translates to: Those who do good deeds will never face ruin.

The underlying message here is clear: when you engage in righteous actions, the universe itself supports your self-confidence.

4. The Union of Motivation and Self-Confidence

If motivation is the spark that ignites a fire, then self-confidence serves as its sustaining flame.

Motivation alone can be easily extinguished.

Self-confidence by itself may risk stagnation.

However, when these two forces come together, they create the flame of progress and success.

Take Mahatma Gandhi as an example. His inspiration stemmed from the pursuit of truth and non-violence.

His self-confidence was encapsulated in the belief that "Even an unarmed man can shake an empire."

This combination of inspiration and self-assurance mobilized an entire nation towards freedom.

5. The Source of Inspiration and Self-Confidence - Dharma

Sanatan Dharma teaches us that genuine inspiration and self-confidence are nourished solely by Dharma.

Dharma instills the understanding that our lives are meant not just for personal happiness but also for the welfare of society and the nation.

It provides self-confidence by reassuring us that God

supports us as long as we remain on the path of Dharma.

Shloka:

"Sarvadharmaanparityajya maamekam sharanam vraj."

(Bhagavad Gita 18.66)

Meaning: Abandon all other religions and seek refuge in me alone; I will liberate you from your sins.

When we take refuge in God, we cultivate an unshakeable self-confidence that instills the belief that nothing is impossible.

6. Ways to Awaken Inspiration

Satsang and Granth Paath - Read the teachings of great souls.

Meditation and Chanting - Activate your inner energy.

Gratitude - Show appreciation for every small step taken.

For instance, look around at those who have achieved success through their struggles.

When you immerse yourself in daily inspiration, it gradually transforms into self-confidence.

7. Ways to Build Self-Confidence

Positive Speech - Affirm to yourself, "I am capable."

Practice and Patience - Confidence naturally develops through repeated effort.

Acknowledge Small Successes - These prepare you for larger victories ahead.

Service and Sacrifice - Working for others empowers you from within.

8. A Contemporary Example - Narendra Modi

The life of Prime Minister Narendra Modi exemplifies a remarkable blend of inspiration and self-confidence. From being a tea seller to holding the highest office in the nation, his journey reflects not just external challenges but also unwavering inner motivation and confidence.

His self-assurance stems from his commitment to serving both his country and Dharma.

This illustrates how a great goal, inspired by Dharma, can lead to boundless self-confidence.

9. Conclusion - Keeping the Flame Alive

Motivation and self-confidence aren't permanent; they need

to be nurtured each day.

It's much like adding oil to a lamp daily.

If the flame of motivation and self-confidence goes out, the road to success becomes obscured.

Sanatana Dharma reminds us -

"Yada yada hi dharmasya glanirbhavati bharat."

(Gita 4.7)

This means: Whenever there is a decline in Dharma, I will come forth to restore balance.

In the same way, when despair begins to take hold in your life, recalling Dharma can reignite your inner flame of motivation and self-confidence.

10. Final Message

If you understand that motivation helps you begin and self-confidence sees you through to the end, you'll never falter.

Together, motivation and self-confidence will light a lamp within you.

This lamp will guide you toward remarkable success as you follow the path of Dharma.

Chapter 15

Cosmic Energy and the Music of Life

Introduction

When you gaze up at the night sky—the countless stars twinkling, the gentle glow of the moon, the radiant sun, the constant flow of rivers, and the swift movement of the wind—have you ever wondered what powers all this? Is it merely a dance of matter and motion? No! An unseen force drives everything, permeating every particle, atom, life form, and thought.

That force is cosmic energy.

In Sanatana Dharma, it's referred to as life, power, consciousness, and a fragment of the Supreme Being.

This energy creates the true music of life.

1. What is cosmic energy?

It is the force that flows with each breath.

It originates in our thoughts.

It shapes our emotions.

It inspires our actions.

The Upanishads state:

"Prano hi sarvam vashe tishthati."

(Prana controls everything.)

In other words, it is cosmic energy that stabilizes the earth, sets planets in motion, illuminates the sun, and grants consciousness to humanity.

2. Music of Life - Flow of Energy

Picture a Veena.

When its strings are properly tuned, it produces sweet melodies.

But if even one string goes slack, it disrupts the entire harmony.

Likewise, human life acts as an instrument.

When its flow of energy is balanced, life's music is harmonious:

Health flourishes.

Success follows easily.

Peace and love abound.

However, when energy becomes blocked, failure, illness, and sorrow emerge.

3. Connecting with Energy - Meditation and Sadhana

The simplest way to tap into cosmic energy is through meditation.

Yoga Vasishtha states:

"Chittasya Shuddhaye Yogah."

(Yoga is for the purification of the mind.)

With meditation,

the mind stabilizes,

the clamor of thoughts quiets,

and cosmic energy flows in effortlessly.

Just 15 minutes of deep breathing and meditation each day

can unlock that inner energy.

4. The Relationship Between Thought and Energy

Every thought is a wave.

Every emotion is a vibration.

These vibrations resonate in the universe, attracting similar energies.

This explains why mantra chanting, sankalp, and prayer are so powerful:

they purify our thoughts and pave the way for energy.

Sanatan Sutra:

"Yathabhavam Tatphalam."

(As the feeling, so the result.)

5. Science and Cosmic Energy

Modern science supports this notion:

Einstein's equation ($E=mc^2$) shows that matter and energy are fundamentally interconnected.

Quantum Physics reveals that every particle is a wave, and every wave represents a flow of energy.

This mirrors the ancient wisdom that sages understood thousands of years ago—that the universe is not merely composed of matter but is an intricate web of energy.

6. Applying It in Life

Cosmic energy isn't just a philosophical concept; it's a tool for life transformation.

Here are five ways to experience and utilize it:

Pranayama and meditation - balancing energy through breath.

Mantra and sound - activating energy through vibrations.

Seva and love - channeling energy through selfless actions.

Gratitude - opening pathways to energy through thankfulness.

Connecting with nature - immersing yourself in sunlight, water, air, and sky.

7. Success Through Cosmic Energy

When a sadhak or individual connects with this energy:

their memory sharpens,

their concentration deepens,

and their aura brightens.

Success begins to flow more easily.

This is why Mahatmas, Yogis, and great leaders achieve remarkable feats while living in ordinary bodies.

8. Inspiring Incident

A sadhu would rise early each morning to meditate.

People often asked, "Do you receive money, food, or clothing from this?"

With a smile, the sadhu replied, "I gain a power that brings me money, food, and clothing. When I connect with energy, all the forces of the world align in my favor."

9. Message from the Scriptures

From the Bhagavad Gita (18.78):

"Yatra Yogeshwarah Krishna Yatra Partho Dhanurdharah.

Tatra Shrirvijayo Bhootirdhruva Niti-Marmatirmam."

(Wherever Yogeshwara Krishna is and where the practitioner

meditates, success, victory, and strategy are assured.)

In this context, Krishna represents cosmic energy. When you tap into it, success is inevitable.

10. Conclusion: The Music of Life

Dear Reader,

Your life is an instrument.

Cosmic energy is its melody.

If you harbor negative thoughts, the notes will clash.

However, through practice and positivity, that same instrument can produce beautiful music.

The Gita states:

"Anando brahmeti vyajanat."

(Brahma is bliss.)

When you connect with cosmic energy, your life transforms into a harmonious symphony of joy, peace, and success.

Key Takeaways:

Cosmic energy pervades everything—your breath, thoughts,

and actions.

Meditation and pranayama unlock access to it.

Positive thinking and gratitude enhance this energy.

Service and love channel its flow.

The true secret to success lies in connecting with cosmic energy.

Verse:

"Yatha sarvagatam saukshmyadakasham noplipyate.

सर्वर्तवास्थितो देहे तथात्मा नोपलिप्यते॥" (Bhagavad Gita 13.32)

(Just as space is everywhere yet remains unattached to anything, so too does the soul—cosmic energy—exist everywhere without attachment.)

Part IV

Struggle & Self-Mastery

Chapter 16

Struggle – The True Companion of Success

"Struggle is the teacher that uncovers a person's strength and true potential."

Introduction

Every significant achievement in history carries with it an untold story of struggle. No individual, no nation, and no civilization has ever reached greatness without enduring the trials of adversity. Struggle is not merely an obstacle on the path to success; it serves as the essential bridge that guides us toward it.

When a seed forces its way through the dark soil to embrace the sunlight, that is a form of struggle. When a river carves valleys through solid rock, that is also struggle. Nature teaches us that growth, transformation, and genuine progress arise only from challenges.

Therefore, we must learn to appreciate our struggles, for they are not punishments but rather opportunities – opportunities to awaken our inner strength, patience, and wisdom.

1. The Importance of Struggle

Struggle serves many purposes in our lives. It shapes our character, fortifies our willpower, and adds depth to our achievements. Without struggle, success remains empty, akin to fruit lacking sweetness.

(a) Spiritual Development

Struggles expose our inner selves. When challenges emerge, we confront our limitations—fear, doubt, and hesitation. Yet simultaneously, we uncover our hidden strengths—courage, creativity, and resilience. This self-awareness represents spiritual growth as it aligns us with the fundamental truth that life is a journey of evolution.

(b) Courage and Patience

In challenging times, two virtues stand out—courage and patience. Courage empowers us to stand firm when everything seems to be falling apart, while patience reminds us that no winter lasts forever. Together, they form the twin pillars that support us as we navigate storms toward calmness and clarity.

(c) Foundation of Success

Every authentic success carries a narrative of struggle behind it. Without this backdrop, accomplishments are fragile and fleeting. Success that comes too easily can lead to arrogance; in contrast, success forged through hardship remains rooted in humility and gratitude.

Proverb:

"Where there are difficulties lies the hidden seed of success."

2. The Story of a Farmer: Ramlal's Perseverance

Stories often convey truths more effectively than theories.

In a small village, there lived a farmer named Ramlal. Farming was not merely his job; it was his passion and way of life. However, fate tested him with ongoing challenges.

In his first year, a severe drought left his fields desolate.

In the second year, pests devastated the few crops he had managed to plant.

By the third year, a sudden flood swept away all his hard work.

Three years of setbacks would have shattered the spirit of an ordinary person. The villagers advised him:

"Ramlal, it's time to give up farming. Luck isn't on your side. Consider doing something else."

But Ramlal responded with unwavering resolve:

"Failure won't stop me; it simply points me toward new possibilities."

Instead of giving in, he transformed each setback into an opportunity for growth:

He analyzed the soil and learned its requirements.

He invested in high-quality seeds.

He ensured timely fertilizers and irrigation were in place.

He embraced new technologies for his fields.

Gradually, his efforts paid off. In the following season, his crops thrived beyond imagination. Golden fields of grain swayed in the breeze, and his storage barns overflowed. The same villagers who once ridiculed him now held him in high regard.

Ramlal's journey imparts a profound lesson: with patience, innovation, and relentless improvement, even repeated failures can become stepping stones to success.

3. Struggle and Mental Strength

Struggle is not merely an external challenge; it is fundamentally an internal trial. It trains the mind to remain calm, focused, and resilient.

Patience: When immediate results are elusive, patience empowers us to persist without losing hope.

Tolerance: Struggles cultivate our ability to endure criticism, delays, and discomfort.

Decision-making: Difficulties compel us to think clearly, evaluate options, and make sound choices.

A person who has never faced struggle is like a sword that has never been honed – it may shine brightly but lacks the ability to cut through obstacles.

Aphorism:

"Struggle is life's iron; only through tempering does it transform into the gold of success."

4. Science and Struggle

Contemporary research also highlights the importance of struggle in personal development.

1. Neuroscience: Studies indicate that when we confront challenges, our brains create new neural connections. This enhances learning, memory, and problem-solving skills. Struggle literally rewires the brain for growth.

2. Energy Science: Struggle produces both mental and physical energy. When faced with challenges, adrenaline heightens our senses and prepares us for action. This elevated state fosters creativity and innovation.

3. Spiritual Vision: From a broader perspective, every struggle aligns us with universal laws. Just as pressure turns coal into diamonds, challenges refine our souls and bring us

closer to harmony with cosmic principles.

5. Exercises & Worksheets - Turning Struggles into Opportunities

To put these lessons into practice, here are some exercises:

1. Conflict Inventory

   List your past and present struggles.

Reflect on the lessons each taught you.

2. Conflict Analysis

   Determine what each challenge revealed to you.

   Ask yourself: "What opportunity was concealed within this difficulty?"

3. Patience & Courage Exercises

   Practice staying calm in stressful situations.

   Establish daily habits like deep breathing, journaling, or meditation.

4. Positive Affirmation

   Repeat daily:

   "I have the strength to face challenges and turn them into opportunities."

These practices train the mind to view obstacles as stepping stones rather than threats.

6. Motivational Quotes on Struggle

"The taste of success is incomplete without struggle."

"Diamonds are formed under pressure; so are resilient souls."

"Only those who confront difficulties achieve lasting success and balance in life."

7. Conclusion

Struggle is not an enemy; it is our greatest ally on the road to success.

1. It is unavoidable; no one can escape it.
2. It serves as a pathway for growth—mental, emotional, and spiritual.
3. It teaches us to see every obstacle as an opportunity.
4. Those who embrace struggle with patience and courage find lasting success and profound fulfillment.

Ultimately, struggle is not just about enduring hardships—it's about transforming through them. It's the unseen companion accompanying every successful person, guiding them toward their true potential.

Remember: The more intense the struggle, the brighter the success that follows.

Chapter 17
Obstacles and Solutions on the Path of Dharma

Introduction: Why do obstacles arise?

When a seeker embarks on the path of Dharma, striving for success and truth while uncovering the secrets of cosmic energy, life inevitably presents tests.

Obstacles are not merely hindrances; they serve as signs that you are on the right track.

Recall the verse from gita-

"क्लेशोऽधिकतरस्तेषामव्यक्तासक्तचेतसाम्।

अव्यक्ता हि गतिर्दुःखं देहवद्भिरवाप्यते॥"

(Gita 12.5)

This means that for those traversing an unseen path, initial challenges are natural, yet these very obstacles can elevate them to greater heights.

Major obstacles on the path of Dharma

Five Primary Obstacles on the Path of Dharma and Success

Every seeker pursuing the path of Dharma and striving for genuine success must confront and overcome certain internal barriers. These obstacles are not external foes but subtle forces within, testing one's resolve and guiding one's growth. Among them, five stand out as the most common and powerful:

1. Ignorance - When someone forgets or fails to acknowledge their own divine potential, they remain confined by limitations. Ignorance obscures their inner strength, wisdom, and abilities, leaving them reliant on external validation instead of awakening the power that already resides within.

2. Fear - Fear takes shape as persistent worry—fear of failure, judgment, or loss. It immobilizes action and hinders one from taking the necessary steps toward success. Fear constructs imaginary barriers in the mind, making challenges seem far larger than they actually are.

3. Attachment - A strong clinging to outcomes, possessions, or relationships traps the seeker. When attachment is present, setbacks lead to despair, while achievements bring anxiety about losing them. This fixation narrows one's focus away from the greater purpose of Dharma and towards fleeting gains.

4. Doubt - The inner voice of uncertainty poses questions like "Am I on the right path? Do I have what it takes? Will I ever succeed?" Doubt undermines faith and drains energy, scattering the mind and stalling progress before it can flourish.

5. Ego - The most subtle and perilous obstacle, ego fosters an illusion of absolute self-importance—believing "I alone am the doer; I control everything." Ego disconnects one from humility, grace, and higher universal forces. When left unchecked, it isolates the seeker and ultimately leads to downfall.

These five obstacles are universal in nature. However, once identified, they can be transformed. Ignorance can yield to knowledge, fear can be met with courage, attachment can

shift to detachment, doubt can give way to faith, and ego can be dissolved through surrender. Overcoming these challenges is not just about attaining external success but also about aligning one's life with Dharma—the eternal principles of truth, balance, and harmony.

These five barriers can impede a seeker's progress.

Solutions - The Religious Perspective

The path of Dharma is not without its challenges, but each challenge holds a key to liberation. The timeless wisdom of religion teaches us how to turn our inner struggles into opportunities for growth.

1. Ignorance → Knowledge

Ignorance casts a shadow over the light of truth. The antidote is genuine knowledge—the insights from scriptures, the guidance of a Guru, and the practice of self-inquiry.

The Upanishads implore: "तमसो मा ज्योतिर्गमय" — "Lead me from darkness to light."

When ignorance fades away, the seeker uncovers their own divine essence and realizes that the power they sought externally has always been within.

2. Fear → Faith

Fear stems from forgetting the Divine. Its remedy is faith—a steadfast trust that God and the universe are constantly supporting your journey.

As stated in the Bible: "When I am afraid, I put my trust in You." (Psalm 56:3)

And Krishna reassures in the Gita: "Mā śucah" – "Do not fear."

With faith, a trembling heart becomes courageous, transforming every challenge into a step toward destiny.

3. Attachment → Dispassion

Attachment ties the soul to temporary pleasures and outcomes. The solution lies in vairagya—holy detachment.

The Gita teaches: "Karmanyevadhikaraste ma phaleshu kadachana" – "You have the right to action, but never to its fruits."

Buddha reminds us: "Attachment is the root of suffering."

When seekers learn to act with devotion while letting go of attachment to results, they find a rare freedom—a joy that remains steady regardless of gain or loss.

4. Doubt → Sadhana

Doubt clouds the mind and scatters energy. Its remedy is sadhana—dedicated practice of meditation, prayer, and devotion.

The Gita states: "The doubting soul perishes; neither this world nor the next nor happiness is for one who doubts." (4.40)

Through sadhana, the fog of doubt lifts, allowing seekers to experience an unbroken flow of inner strength. Faith replaces confusion, illuminating their path with clarity.

5. Ego → Surrender

Ego poses as the greatest barrier, insisting "I am the doer." Its remedy is surrender—the relinquishing of one's false self at the feet of the Divine.

As Kabir expressed: "When 'I' was present, God was not; now that God is here, I am not."

The Gita also affirms: "Offer all that you do to Me… with your mind focused on the Self, free from ego and longing; be ever content." (9.27)

When surrender blossoms, the seeker becomes an instrument of the Divine will. Life flows effortlessly, and success, peace, and grace naturally manifest.

Short story: River and stone

A devotee asked the Guru, "Gurudev, I follow the path of religion but keep stopping. Why is that?"

The Guru smiled and replied, "Observe the river. When it encounters stones in its way, it doesn't stop. Instead, it either carves through them or alters its course to keep flowing. A seeker should be like the river. Obstacles arise only to deepen your experience."

Self-introspection formula

An obstacle is not an enemy; it's a hidden teacher.

If you face no difficulties on your journey, it means you are stagnant rather than progressing.

Obstacles along the path of Dharma exist to elevate you from the ordinary to the extraordinary.

Exercise / Worksheet

1. Identify your obstacles:

- Write down three major obstacles that hinder your progress toward your goals.

2. Add the solution formula:

- Next to each obstacle, write down its solution from a Dharma perspective.

3. Daily meditation:

- Spend 10 minutes sitting quietly and repeat this phrase:

"I am a traveler on the path of Dharma; every obstacle is making me stronger."

4. Write positive affirmations:

- Examples include: "Fear is merely an illusion," "Truth lies beyond doubt," "I am connected to universal power."

Conclusion

Obstacles do not come to block your path but to prepare you for what lies ahead.

When you walk with Dharma and faith, every challenge transforms into an opportunity for growth.

Remember:

.Obstacle = Sign

.Solution = Sadhana

.Result = Success

Chapter 18
The Power of Restraint and Self-Control

Introduction: The Invisible Weapon of Self-Control

One of life's most challenging tasks is mastering oneself. While great empires have been built, stunning structures erected, and remarkable scientific advancements made, few disciplines are as profound and demanding as self-restraint. Maharishi Patanjali stated in the Yoga Sutras:

"योगश्चित्तवृत्तिनिरोधः"

This translates to: The primary goal of Yoga is to calm the restless mind and exercise restraint.

Restraint involves more than just suppressing desires or passions; it means harmoniously controlling thoughts, speech, and actions. Self-control is the power that enables a person to discern right from wrong.

Narendra Modi's life vividly illustrates this quality. Despite growing up amid scarcity, these limitations instilled in him a strong sense of discipline and restraint. From an early age, he recognized that achieving something significant in life requires mastery over one's desires rather than becoming enslaved by them.

Restraint: The Source of Power

In Indian philosophy, restraint is viewed as a divine quality. In Chapter 6 of the Bhagavad Gita, Lord Krishna tells Arjuna –

"उद्धरेदात्मनात्मानं नात्मानमवसादयेत्। आत्मैव ह्यात्मनो बन्धुरात्मैव रिपुरात्मनः॥"

This means: A person can be both their own friend and their own enemy. When one gains control over their mind, they become their greatest ally; when they lose that control, they become their greatest foe.

Restraint does not merely suppress desires; it channels them in the right direction. It is like fire – when harnessed properly, it provides warmth; when left unchecked, it can consume everything in its path.

Self-Restraint in Modi Ji's Life

Numerous examples of restraint can be seen throughout Narendra Modi's life:

1. Restraint in Personal Life - Even after becoming Prime Minister, Modi Ji continues to lead a life marked by simplicity and discipline. He avoids luxury and personal indulgence, opting instead for simple meals and a strict routine.
2. Restraint in Speech - In the political arena where harsh language and personal attacks often prevail, Modi Ji frequently displays restraint in his communication. He understands that even under pressure, careful word choice is essential.
3. Control over Anger - Despite facing harsh criticism and opposition, he seldom shows anger

publicly. This self-control allows him to remain balanced and resilient as a leader.

The Scientific Perspective of Restraint

Modern science has increasingly validated what ancient Indian wisdom has always emphasized—that self-control is one of the most important predictors of success, health, and happiness.

One of the most famous studies in psychology, popularly known as the Stanford Marshmallow Experiment, provides powerful evidence of this truth. In the late 1960s and early 1970s, psychologist Walter Mischel and his team conducted an experiment with preschool children. Each child was offered a choice: they could eat one marshmallow immediately, or wait for about 15 minutes and then receive two marshmallows as a reward.

What the researchers observed was remarkable. Some children gave in quickly and ate the marshmallow, unable to resist the temptation. Others struggled, distracting themselves by singing, covering their eyes, or looking away, but managed to wait and earned the larger reward.

The real significance of this experiment came years later. When researchers followed up with these children as teenagers and adults, they discovered a striking pattern. Those who had demonstrated self-control by delaying gratification:

Performed better academically and scored higher on standardized tests.

Had healthier body weight and were less prone to obesity.

Showed stronger coping skills in dealing with stress.

Developed more stable relationships and higher levels of self-confidence.

Were less likely to fall into substance abuse or impulsive behavior.

In contrast, the children who had eaten the marshmallow immediately tended to struggle more with impulse control, faced academic difficulties, and reported higher levels of frustration in adulthood.

Subsequent studies in neuroscience have further revealed that self-control is linked to the prefrontal cortex, the part of the brain responsible for decision-making, planning, and regulating behavior. Strengthening this "mental muscle" of self-restraint not only influences short-term discipline but also long-term success.

Thus, science confirms what the scriptures have long taught: the ability to postpone immediate gratification, restrain impulses, and direct energy wisely is not just a moral virtue but a psychological strength. Restraint ensures not only external achievements—such as career growth and social recognition—but also inner fulfillment, peace of mind, and overall well-being.

Self-Control Cultivates Inner Strength

True strength isn't found in physical might or external possessions; it resides in self-mastery. Restraint serves as a hidden force, protecting individuals from harmful temptations while directing their inner energy toward meaningful purposes and positive outcomes. When someone learns to control their thoughts, words, and actions, they tap into a wellspring of inner strength that forms the basis of success, dignity, and peace.

1. Restraint in Speech - A Route to Respect

Words can heal or harm, build or destroy. A single thoughtless word spoken in anger can fracture relationships built over years, whereas a kind and thoughtful word can win hearts in an instant.

Those who practice restraint in their speech earn the trust and respect of others.

Leaders, saints, and visionaries throughout history are remembered not for how loudly they spoke but for the depth and wisdom of their words.

Narendra Modi often exemplifies this—choosing his words with care, understanding their impact on millions, and demonstrating that self-control in speech is a hallmark of true leadership.

2. Restraint of the Senses - Protecting Against Decline

Unbridled indulgence of the senses leads to dependency, distraction, and moral decline. Whether it's overeating, seeking constant comfort, or becoming attached to material pleasures, unchecked senses can imprison a person.

Restraint doesn't imply denial but rather balance—enjoying food in moderation, prioritizing timely sleep, and living with discipline.

Research shows that individuals who practice sensory restraint tend to enjoy better health, sharper focus, and increased productivity.

By safeguarding the senses, one protects their character and paves a steady path toward growth rather than decline.

3. Restraint in Thoughts - Cultivating Positivity and Creativity

Every action starts as a thought. When thoughts are negative, restless, or destructive, they eventually show up in words and actions that reflect the same negativity.

A disciplined mind learns to reject harmful thoughts and instead focuses on positive, constructive ideas.

This mindset fosters creativity, encourages problem-solving, and builds resilience during challenging times.

Great thinkers like Swami Vivekananda highlighted that

controlling one's thoughts is the highest form of strength because it directs the limitless potential of the human mind toward noble endeavors.

4. Restraint in Actions - Building an Admirable Character

Actions serve as the true measure of a person's character. While one may think or speak wisely, it is through actions that genuine discipline is revealed.

Someone who controls their impulses and acts only after careful thought naturally becomes a role model for others.

Such restraint ensures that actions align with values rather than fleeting emotions.

Over time, principled actions foster a reputation for integrity and inspire trust, forming the foundation of both leadership and personal relationships.

In this sense, self-control is not a limitation but rather a liberation. It frees an individual from the shackles of impulses and channels energy toward higher goals. It becomes a quiet power that shapes destiny. As Mahatma Gandhi once said, "The control of the palate is the first essential in the observance of the vow of self-restraint." When this principle extends to speech, senses, thoughts, and actions, it empowers an individual—powerful not over others, but over oneself.

Inspirational Examples

1. Mahatma Gandhi - His commitment to celibacy and a disciplined lifestyle formed the bedrock of his inner strength.
2. Swami Vivekananda - He asserted that there is no greater power than self-restraint, emphasizing that spiritual growth can only be achieved through self-control.
3. Narendra Modi - His rise from a humble background to the position of Prime Minister exemplifies the transformative power of restraint and self-discipline.

The Importance of Restraint in Today's Society

Modern society leans heavily toward consumerism, indulgence, and distraction. Young people often find themselves caught up in fleeting pleasures and temptations. In this context, teaching restraint and self-control becomes increasingly vital.

Restraint not only contributes to personal success but also fosters balance, peace, and morality within society.

Conclusion: Restraint is the Key to Success

The strength of restraint and self-control originates from within; it is a discipline that requires ongoing practice. The life of Narendra Modi exemplifies that true leadership can only be achieved through self-control.

Message:

If you aspire to achieve great heights in life, focus on disciplining your mind. Manage your desires, speak kindly, and regulate your behavior. In doing so, you will uncover the inner strength that guides you toward genuine success.

Chapter 19
The Attraction of Love and Compassion

"अहिंसा परमो धर्मः, करुणा परमः शक्तिः।"

— महर्षि व्यास

Introduction

Why Love and Compassion are the Greatest Laws of Attraction

Among all the principles that govern life and creation, love

stands out as the most ancient, powerful, and universal. It serves as the eternal thread connecting stars, planets, and every living being into a unified whole. Without love, creation, harmony, and life itself cannot exist.

Compassion naturally arises from love. While love encourages gentleness, compassion instills courage—the courage to share in the pain of others and strive for their betterment. Love is the seed, and compassion is the tree that grows from it.

The "Law of Attraction" reaches its fullest expression when intertwined with love and compassion. Simply wanting something does not bring success; rather, it is the purity of heart that truly attracts it. Saints, sages, and great leaders have consistently imparted this fundamental truth –

"Love all, serve all, and have compassion for all. This is the true path to fulfillment."

1. The Energy of Love and Its Magnetism

Love is more than just an emotion; it's a gentle vibration that emanates from the heart. While we can't measure these vibrations with conventional tools, their effects are undeniably significant.

When a person is filled with love, their presence becomes magnetic. Those around them feel a sense of calm and joy.

Compassion radiates from individuals, making even animals, children, and strangers feel safe in their company.

The universe also acknowledges this energy. A decision made with love and compassion returns with even greater force.

Example: A teacher who educates with love inspires students who excel not only in knowledge but also in character. A leader who guides with compassion earns not just authority but also the admiration of countless people.

Thus, love is not a sign of weakness; it represents the ultimate power of attraction.

2. Compassion - The Greatest Language of the Soul

Compassion (करुणा) is the most profound expression of love. It goes beyond pity; it involves actively engaging in another's joys and sorrows.

To experience compassion means to feel the pain of others as if it were your own.

To act compassionately means standing alongside someone in their struggles and providing them support.

Buddha stated:

"धर्म बिना करुणा अधूरा है।"

("Religion is incomplete without compassion.")

Practicing compassion purifies our minds. Negative emotions like ego, jealousy, and hatred begin to fade away. A compassionate heart reflects divinity—resolutions formed within it are naturally fulfilled.

3. The Law of Love and Attraction

The Law of Attraction asserts that whatever energy we project into the universe will return to us. When this energy is filled with love and compassion, it becomes irresistible.

Someone who genuinely wishes well for others unknowingly draws goodwill and positive circumstances into their own life.

A person who serves society with compassion finds that challenges effortlessly dissipate from their path.

While a selfish resolution may or may not succeed, one born out of compassion will always prevail.

Formula for Success:

Resolution + Love + Compassion = Unstoppable Attraction

4. Stories - The Power of Love and Compassion

(a) Mahatma Gandhi and the Appeal of Compassion

Gandhiji's life served as a powerful example of compassion in action. He consistently rejected violence, even when faced with the formidable British Empire. His deep empathy for the oppressed became his greatest strength. As a result, he earned the title of Mahatma from people around the world, and his compassion-driven movement liberated millions without resorting to hatred or warfare.

(b) The Impact of an Ordinary Woman

In a small village, a impoverished woman made it her mission to educate children who had no access to schooling. With patience, love, and compassion, she taught them every day. Over time, these children grew into responsible adults—teachers, doctors, and leaders. The entire village underwent a transformation thanks to one woman's compassionate efforts.

These stories illustrate that compassion isn't exclusive to saints or leaders; even everyday individuals can change the world through love.

5. Scientific Insights on Compassion

Modern science now validates what ancient sages in India have long understood: compassion not only enriches the soul but also benefits the body.

Heart health: Compassion alleviates stress and helps stabilize heart rates.

Immunity: Practices rooted in loving-kindness boost the immune system.

Hormones: The brain releases oxytocin (the Love Hormone), which decreases anxiety and fosters trust.

Relationships: Those who are compassionate tend to form stronger, healthier social connections.

Thus, compassion emerges as both a spiritual principle and a biological necessity for true happiness.

6. The Balance of Religion, Love, and Success

Religion teaches us that success devoid of love is meaningless and that power lacking compassion can be destructive.

A wealthy individual without compassion feels empty inside.

A powerful leader who lacks love risks becoming a tyrant.

However, a leader who merges strength with compassion leaves an enduring legacy in history.

True success is guided by love and compassion.

7. Practical Exercises and Workbook

Exercise 1 - Compassion Meditation

Take 10 minutes each day to sit quietly and repeat this thought: "May all beings be happy. May all beings be free from suffering. May all beings be blessed with peace." This meditation cleanses the heart and fills it with uplifting energy.

Exercise 2 - Daily Acts of Love

Make it a daily practice to offer love or assistance to at least one person without expecting anything in return. This can include:

Feeding someone who is hungry.

Comforting someone who is grieving.

Sharing a smile with a stranger.

Exercise 3 - Compassion Journal

Every night, take a moment to write in your journal:

Who did I show compassion to today?

Did I provide love and support to anyone?

What was the impact on me and the other person?

This routine gradually fosters a compassionate character.

8. Sutra

Love represents the greatest law of the universe.

Compassion speaks the deepest language of the soul.

The more love and compassion you share, the more abundantly the universe responds in kind.

9. Conclusion

This chapter illustrates that true success cannot stem solely from desires. It requires the pure energy of love and compassion. Love connects us, while compassion lifts us up.

A life guided by love and compassion becomes not only appealing but also transcendent. It has the power to transform individuals, communities, and nations.

Therefore, choose the path of love, practice compassion each day, and watch as the universe opens doors to success, peace, and lasting fulfillment for you.

Chapter 20
The Union of Religion, Science, and Attraction

Introduction: Not Opposition, but Complementarity

It is a common misconception that religion and science stand in opposition to one another. While science seeks truth in laboratories and religion finds it in temples or places of meditation, the reality is that both are different pathways leading to the same truth.

Religion states:

"सत्यं वद। धर्मं चर। स्वाध्यायान्मा प्रमदः॥"

This means speaking the truth and practicing righteousness. Religion is not merely a form of worship; it embodies moral values, ethics, and our responsibilities.

Science asserts:

"Observe, experiment, and conclude."

When the principles of religion are merged with the laws of science alongside the principle of attraction, individuals can achieve not only material success but also spiritual fulfillment.

1. View of Religion: The Eternal Principle of Attraction

Indian sages proclaimed thousands of years ago:

"यद्भावं तद्भवति।"

(As is the feeling, so is the future.)

In essence, what you focus on in your mind shapes your reality. This represents the Law of Attraction!

Religion teaches that only pure intentions can influence the universe.

The Upanishads convey:

"मनसा भावयति लोकान्।"

(The feeling in the mind creates the world.)

Thus, religion has long suggested that the principle of attraction is not mere fantasy but a fundamental law governing the universe.

2. View of Science: The Dynamics of Energy and Vibration

Science posits that everything in the universe consists of energy.

According to physics:

matter = a compressed form of energy.

In quantum physics:

every particle vibrates continuously.

When we think, our thoughts generate energy waves that ripple through the universe, attracting similar vibrations.

This explains why—

Positive thinking draws positive circumstances.

Negative thinking yields negative outcomes.

This illustrates how science validates the Law of Attraction.

3. Law of Attraction: The Intersection of Dharma and Science

If Dharma asserts that "pure resolve yields results" and Science claims "thoughts are energy," then together they demonstrate that individuals have the power to create their own realities.

Dharma provides us with morality and guidance.

Science offers us logic and evidence.

The Law of Attraction serves as our tool for practice.

Together, these three elements create a holistic path forward.

4. Example: From Ancient Sages to Modern Experiments

Sage Vishwamitra manifested "Trishanku Swarga," a heavenly realm, purely through his determination.

Arjuna discovered the essence of the Gita by channeling his focus and purpose on the battlefield.

In contemporary science, the quantum double-slit experiment demonstrates that

the observer's perspective influences a particle's behavior.

Is this not what Dharma refers to as "emotion and resolution"?

5. Application in Life: Dharma + Science + Attraction

(a) Health

Dharma: Pure food, yoga, and prayer

Science: A balanced diet, exercise, and insights from neuroscience

Attraction: Healthy thoughts and visualization positively impact body cells.

(b) Relationships

Dharma: Compassion, truth, and forgiveness

Science: Principles from psychology and neuroscience

Attraction: Sharing the energy of love and harmony.

(c) Success

Dharma: Actions aligned with Dharma

Science: Setting goals and putting in effort

Attraction: Embracing feelings and visualizing "I am successful," which draws in opportunities.

6. Sadhana and Discipline

Religion teaches that mere wishing won't yield results; dedication and discipline are essential.

Science supports this by stating that continuous practice—

not just imagination—alters the brain's neural pathways.

Thus –

The Law of Attraction functions effectively only when paired with spiritual commitment and consistent practice.

7. Shloka Inspiration

The Gita states:

"श्रद्धावान् लभते ज्ञानं तत्परः संयतेन्द्रियः।

ज्ञानं लब्ध्वा परां शान्तिमचिरेणाधिगच्छति॥"

(Knowledge and rewards come through faith.)

This implies that science, rooted in skepticism alone, is incomplete, just as religion grounded solely in superstition falls short.

A balance of both faith and discernment is crucial.

8. Workbook / Exercise (for the reader)

1. Meditation

Spend 10 minutes each day sitting quietly with your eyes closed.

Repeat this positive affirmation:

"I am attracting a religious, healthy, and successful life."

2. Visualization Practice

Create a vivid mental image of your goal (either in your mind or written down).

From a scientific perspective: This activates the brain's reticular activating system.

3. Dharma-Based Resolution

Before setting any goal, ask yourself:

"Is this goal aligned with Dharma?"

If it is, then both the law of attraction and scientific principles will work together to support you.

4. Balance of Science and Religion

Dedicate half an hour to studying science followed by half an hour on religious texts.

Feed your mind from both perspectives.

Conclusion

Religion, science, and attraction are all distinct expressions of the same truth.

Religion offers us guidance.

Science provides evidence.

Attraction gives us the tools we need.

By harmonizing these three elements, one can attain not only material success but also spiritual tranquility in life.

Chapter 21
From Mystery to Success

1. Introduction: The Last Stop of the Journey

Every journey has a starting point and an end. This book's journey was a quest to uncover the hidden truths of religion, spirituality, and manifestation that can transform an ordinary life into something extraordinary.

At first, for those on this path, everything feels like a mystery. Their focus is often on the material world, preventing them from seeing the deeper truths that lie within their souls.

However, as the seeker progresses, they begin to understand that the "secret" isn't an external force but rather the dormant consciousness residing inside them.

Only when this consciousness awakens does true success emerge—not just in terms of wealth or status but in achieving balance, peace, and a sense of divinity.

2. What is the Mystery?

In the Sanatan tradition, mystery refers to an "unrevealed truth." It's something that remains invisible to many despite being right in front of them.

Lord Shri Krishna conveys this in the Geeta:

"इदं तु ते गुह्यतम प्रवक्ष्यम्यंसुयवे।

(गीता 9.1)

Good luck with knowledge and science, yajnyatva and salvation.

This signifies that this ultimate secret can only be grasped by those with sincere intentions.

The Upanishads describe this mystery as "Brahma Vidya" –

"Satyam Gyanmanantam Brahma" – this is Brahma; it is the

supreme mystery.

From a modern perspective, this mystery can be viewed as:

- Planning mental energy,

- Clarity of resolution,

- Consistency in action.

Together, these three elements open doors to success.

3. Definition of Success: Beyond Material Wealth

In today's society, success is often narrowly defined by money, position, and fame. However, from a Sanatan viewpoint, true success encompasses:

1. Spiritual success - self-recognition.
2. Social success - contributing positively to society.
3. Material success - ethical use of resources.
4. Spiritual success - establishing a connection with God.

A balance among these four aspects constitutes what we can call "complete success."

4. Sadhana: From Mystery to Success

(a) Mind - The Power of Thought

The mind serves as the source of resolutions and thoughts.

When negativity clouds the mind, it hampers one's resolve.

Conversely, with a pure and clear mind, every goal becomes attainable.

In the Gita, Shri Krishna states:

"उद्धरेदात्मनात्मानं नात्मानमवसादयेत्।"

which means—one should elevate oneself rather than succumb to despair.

(b) Speech - the foundation of truth

Speech goes beyond mere communication; it embodies vibration. When a seeker speaks with sincerity, their words become Brahman.

The essence of the mind is unveiled through speech.

(c) Karma - Dharma-oriented work

Simply thinking and speaking are not enough.

Success can only be achieved when resolve is transformed into action.

Only work aligned with Dharma leads to lasting success; otherwise, achievements remain fleeting.

5. Historical and contemporary examples

(a) Shri Krishna

He revealed Dharma in a profound manner to Arjuna.

His success extended beyond winning the Mahabharata; it was about restoring Dharma.

(b) Chanakya

He transformed an ordinary boy, Chandragupta, into an emperor.

His secret lay in blending politics with Dharma-oriented principles.

(c) Swami Vivekananda

He shared the essence of self-confidence and Vedanta with the world.

His success was in revitalizing the spirit of India.

(d) Narendra Modi

The key to his journey lies in patience, perseverance, and a commitment to Dharma.

He elevated success beyond politics to shape "India's global identity."

6. The connection between religion and success

Success without religion resembles a sandcastle—it crumbles at the first wave.

However, when success is rooted in religion, it becomes enduring.

This is why the path to success in the Gita is portrayed as selfless Karmayoga.

“कर्मण्येवाधिकारस्ते मा फलेषु कदाचन।”

7. Practice: Your secret, your success

Workbook Practice

1. What is my most significant life resolution?

(Write it down clearly)

2. What small actions can I take each day to turn my resolution into reality?

3. Is my definition of success purely personal or does it also connect to society and the nation?

4. Spend 10 minutes each day in silence and write –

How well have I understood my secret today?

How much progress have I made toward success today?

8. Inspirational Conclusion

The core message of this entire journey is that the "secret" resides not outside but within us.

When we acknowledge it, practice it, and translate it into success through the path of Dharma –

only then does life attain its fullness.

This journey from mystery to success truly takes us

"from ignorance to knowledge, from falsehood to truth, and from death to immortality."

Final Message

Dear Sadhak,

The path you've traveled thus far represents not just a truth to read but one worth living out.

If you practice a little bit every day, this secret will become a

part of your soul and success will come to your feet on its own.

Conclusion

Dharma Path: The Secret Way to Manifestation

A person's life journey is not solely driven by desires and aspirations; it also involves a profound spiritual path that provides direction. In this book, we have sought to uncover that very path—the path of Dharma—where manifestation transcends mere material success and evolves into a process of spiritual fulfillment.

By understanding the essence of manifestation, we discover that it isn't an external force but arises from the purity of our thoughts, the sanctity of our feelings, and the righteousness of our actions. When a person aligns their mind, speech, and actions with the principles of religion, only then do their desires come to fruition and create extraordinary outcomes in life.

The Sanatan tradition teaches us that religion is not confined to worship alone; it embodies the principles of balance, duty, and truth in every aspect of life. If we plant the seed of manifestation in this light, it can grow into a tree that enriches our existence.

Dear reader, this book aims not just to impart knowledge but also to inspire you to recognize your inner power—the very force capable of transforming any situation in your life. The journey ahead lies in your hands.

You will be guided by your own thoughts, resolutions, and beliefs.

Remember—

1. When you define your goals,
2. When you let go of negativity,
3. When you act in accordance with Dharma,
4. The entire universe aligns with you to turn your desires into reality.

Practice and Life Transformation

Knowledge without practice is like an unlit lamp—full of

potential but unable to shine. The true brilliance of manifestation and Dharma emerges not from theory but through lived experience. It is the daily discipline that bridges the gap between what we know and who we become. Practice is the transformative process that turns wisdom into reality.

Every thought you nurture is a seed of destiny. Each word you speak carries vibration. Every action you take either elevates your spirit or confines you within limitations. By consciously practicing clarity of vision, nurturing positive affirmations, engaging in meditation, expressing gratitude, and embracing selfless service, you begin to plant seeds that will inevitably bloom into abundance.

Transformation is never accidental; it is a conscious choice. It arises from persistence, patience, and faith. Just as a river carves valleys through its continuous flow, practice reshapes your life into a masterpiece of balance, prosperity, and inner harmony.

A truly transformed life is measured not only by external accomplishments but also by inner peace. It shows itself in a calmness that no storm can disrupt, in relationships rooted in trust and love, and in contributions that uplift communities and heal divisions. Such a life extends beyond the self—it becomes an offering to the Divine, a flame illuminating the path for others.

Ultimately, manifestation isn't about forcing the universe to cater to your desires; it's about aligning your will with the cosmic order. When this harmony is achieved, resistance fades away. Life begins to flow effortlessly toward its destination. In this state, you don't chase your dreams—they come to you naturally because they are expressions of your highest self.

This captures the essence of transformation: living in harmony with Dharma, embodying the truths you've discovered, and allowing your life itself to stand as the greatest testament to manifestation.

As we conclude this book, I encourage you to embrace the path of Dharma in all areas of your life and make this secret route to manifestation your steadfast companion.

May your life be filled with light, balance, and achievement.

Lalit 'Nambardar'